SECTOR ROTATION STRATEGIES

Mastering The Economic Cycles

By
Dr. Paul .C. Ajulufoh

© 2024 Dr. Paul C. Ajulufoh
All rights reserved.

No part of this book may be reproduced, distributed, or transmitted in any form or by any means without the prior written permission of the author, except in the case of brief quotations embodied in critical reviews and certain other noncommercial uses permitted by copyright law.

ISBN: 979-8334437463

Disclaimer: The information provided in this book is for educational purposes only and does not constitute financial advice. The author is not liable for any losses or damages associated with the use of this book.

Self-published via Amazon Kindle Direct Publishing

TABLE OF CONTENTS

Introduction
- Overview of sector rotation strategies
- Importance of understanding economic cycles
- Brief outline of the book's content

Chapter 1: Understanding Economic Cycles
- Understanding economic cycles
  - Expansion: Characteristics and indicators
  - Peak: Warning signs and market behavior
  - Contraction: Identifying downturns and sector impact
  - Trough: Recovery signals and sector opportunities
- Key economic metrics (GDP, unemployment, inflation)
- Leading, lagging, and coincident indicators

Chapter 2: Sector Classification
- Defining sectors and industries
- Major sectors in the economy
- Tools for sector classification (GICS, ICB, NAICS, SIC)
- Importance of accurate classification

Chapter 3: The Theory Behind Sector Rotation
- Correlation between economic cycles and sector performance
- Historical performance of sectors in different economic phases
- Rationale for rotating sectors

Chapter 4: Implementing Sector Rotation Strategies
- Identifying economic cycle phases
- Choosing sectors to invest in during each phase
- Timing and frequency of rotations
- Practical steps for sector rotation

Chapter 5: Analytical Tools and Indicators
- Key economic indicators to monitor (GDP growth, employment data, inflation rates, consumer confidence, interest rates)
- Technical analysis tools (moving averages, RSI, MACD, support and resistance levels, volume analysis)
- Fundamental analysis for sector evaluation (earnings reports, P/E ratios, industry trends)
- Combining technical and fundamental analysis

Chapter 6: Case Studies
- Detailed case studies of successful sector rotation strategies
- Lessons learned from past economic cycles
- Analysis of real-world examples

Chapter 7: Advanced Techniques
- Combining sector rotation with other strategies (momentum investing, value investing, growth investing)
- Utilizing ETFs and mutual funds for sector rotation
- Risk management and diversification (portfolio diversification, hedging strategies, dynamic asset allocation, stop-loss orders)
- Practical considerations (costs, tax implications, rebalancing, monitoring and adjustments, risk tolerance, time horizon)

Chapter 8: Practical Considerations

- Building and managing a sector rotation portfolio
- Understanding costs and tax implications
- Avoiding common pitfalls (overtrading, ignoring diversification, failing to monitor and adjust, over-reliance on economic indicators, emotional investing)

Chapter 9: Future Trends in Sector Rotation
- Impact of technological advancements (AI and machine learning, big data, automated trading and robo-advisors)
- Increasing importance of sustainability and ESG criteria (ESG integration, impact investing)
- Role of global economic integration (cross-border investments, trade policies and geopolitical risks, technological transfer and innovation)
- Adapting to future trends (embracing technological tools, integrating ESG criteria, considering global perspectives)

Chapter 10: Creating a Sector Rotation Plan
- Setting investment goals and risk tolerance
- Understanding the economic cycle
- Selecting sectors for each phase
- Implementing your strategy (choosing investment vehicles, setting entry and exit points, diversifying your portfolio)
- Monitoring and adjusting your plan (regular portfolio reviews, staying informed, making timely adjustments, learning and adapting)
- Risk management and tax considerations

Conclusion
- Recap of key takeaways
- Final thoughts on mastering sector rotation strategies
- Action steps for investors (develop a plan, stay informed,

implement and review)

INTRODUCTION

Overview of Sector Rotation Strategies

Sector rotation is an advanced investment strategy that involves shifting investments between different sectors of the economy to capitalize on the cyclical nature of economic growth. By understanding which sectors perform best during different phases of the economic cycle, investors can potentially enhance their returns and reduce risks.

The concept of sector rotation is rooted in the understanding that the economy goes through various phases—expansion, peak, contraction, and trough—each impacting different sectors uniquely. For instance, technology and consumer discretionary sectors might thrive during an expansion, while utilities and consumer staples might perform better during a contraction.

- **Expansion Phase**: This is characterized by increasing economic activity, rising GDP, and generally improving business conditions. During this phase, growth-oriented sectors like technology and consumer discretionary often perform well as consumers and businesses spend more.
- **Peak Phase**: Economic activity is at its highest point, and inflationary pressures might build. Defensive sectors like healthcare and utilities may start to outperform as growth sectors become overvalued.
- **Contraction Phase**: Economic activity slows down, and recessionary pressures may take hold. Defensive sectors typically continue to perform well, while cyclical sectors such as industrials and consumer discretionary may underperform.

- **Trough Phase**: The economy hits the lowest point of the cycle and starts to recover. Early cyclical sectors such as financials and consumer discretionary may begin to outperform in anticipation of recovery.

By strategically rotating investments into sectors that are expected to outperform during specific economic phases, investors can potentially optimize their portfolio performance.

Importance and Relevance in Current Economic Scenarios

In today's volatile market, characterized by rapid technological advancements, geopolitical tensions, and unprecedented events like the COVID-19 pandemic, sector rotation offers a dynamic approach to investing. Traditional buy-and-hold strategies may not suffice in such an environment, making sector rotation an attractive alternative.

Several factors underscore the importance and relevance of sector rotation strategies in the current economic scenario:

- **Market Volatility**: Frequent shifts in market sentiment and economic indicators necessitate a flexible investment approach. Sector rotation allows investors to adapt to changing conditions.
- **Technological Advancements**: Rapid innovations can cause significant shifts in sector performance. For instance, the rise of e-commerce has propelled the technology and consumer discretionary sectors.
- **Geopolitical Tensions**: Political instability and trade tensions can impact certain sectors more than others. Sector rotation helps in mitigating risks associated with such events.
- **Economic Disruptions**: Events like the COVID-19 pandemic have led to abrupt economic changes, impacting various sectors differently. Understanding and anticipating these impacts can enhance investment decisions.

Investors who can accurately identify economic phases and

align their portfolios accordingly stand to gain significantly. This strategy not only helps in maximizing returns but also in mitigating risks associated with market downturns. Given the limited coverage of this topic in existing literature, this book aims to fill the gap by providing comprehensive insights and practical guidance on implementing sector rotation strategies effectively.

Objectives of the Book

This book aims to:

1. **Educate readers about the fundamentals of sector rotation strategies**: We will delve into the principles of sector rotation, explaining how economic cycles influence sector performance and why understanding these relationships is crucial for investors.
2. **Provide detailed analysis and practical tools for implementing these strategies**: The book will offer in-depth analysis of historical data, practical tools for economic forecasting, and methodologies for selecting sectors during different economic phases.
3. **Offer real-world case studies and advanced techniques for experienced investors**: Through case studies and advanced techniques, the book will illustrate how sector rotation has been successfully implemented in the past and how experienced investors can refine their strategies.
4. **Help readers build and manage a sector rotation portfolio**: We will provide step-by-step guidance on constructing and managing a sector rotation portfolio, including considerations for portfolio diversification, risk management, and performance monitoring.
5. **Address practical considerations, including costs, taxes, and common pitfalls**: Practical advice on managing transaction costs, understanding tax implications, and avoiding common mistakes will be covered to ensure readers are well-equipped to

implement sector rotation strategies effectively.

By the end of this book, readers will have a deep understanding of sector rotation and be equipped with the knowledge and tools to apply these strategies to their own investments, enhancing their ability to navigate economic cycles and achieve their financial goals.

CHAPTER 1: UNDERSTANDING ECONOMIC CYCLES

Understanding economic cycles is fundamental to effectively implementing sector rotation strategies. Each phase of the economic cycle affects various sectors differently, providing opportunities and risks for investors. This chapter delves into the phases of the economic cycle, the indicators that signal each phase, and historical examples to illustrate these concepts.

Phases of the Economic Cycle

Economic cycles consist of four main phases: expansion, peak, contraction, and trough. Each phase has distinct characteristics and impacts different sectors of the economy in unique ways. By recognizing and understanding these phases, investors can better position their portfolios to capitalize on opportunities and mitigate risks.

Expansion: Characteristics and Indicators

The expansion phase is characterized by growth in economic activity, driven by increased consumer and business spending.

During this phase, key indicators reflect robust economic health and optimism:

- **Increasing GDP**: A consistent rise in Gross Domestic Product (GDP) indicates that the economy is growing. Businesses expand operations, and production levels increase to meet rising demand.
- **Rising Employment**: Job creation accelerates, leading to lower unemployment rates. More people are employed, resulting in higher household incomes and increased spending.
- **Consumer Spending Growth**: With higher employment and income, consumers feel confident about their financial situation and spend more on goods and services, driving further economic growth.
- **Business Investments**: Companies invest in capital goods, such as machinery, technology, and infrastructure, to expand their operations and improve productivity.

Key Indicators:

- **Retail Sales**: An increase in retail sales reflects higher consumer spending and confidence in the economy.
- **Industrial Production**: Rising industrial production indicates growing manufacturing activity and business expansion.
- **Business Investments**: Increased capital expenditures by businesses signal optimism about future growth prospects.

Sector Performance:

During the expansion phase, specific sectors tend to outperform as economic conditions improve and consumer and business spending increases. Here's a closer look at the sectors that typically thrive during this phase:

- **Technology**: The technology sector often leads during

an expansion due to increased business investments in new technologies and consumer spending on gadgets and digital services. Companies involved in software development, hardware production, and tech services see significant growth as businesses upgrade their infrastructure and consumers buy the latest devices.

- **Consumer Discretionary**: This sector includes businesses that sell non-essential goods and services, such as retail, automotive, and leisure companies. As consumers feel more financially secure, they are more likely to spend on luxury items, travel, and entertainment. Retailers, automakers, and hospitality businesses often report higher revenues and profits during this phase.
- **Industrials**: The industrials sector benefits from increased business activity and capital investments. Companies in this sector, which include construction firms, machinery manufacturers, and transportation providers, experience higher demand as businesses expand operations and invest in new infrastructure. Government spending on infrastructure projects can also boost the industrial sector during an expansion.

By focusing on these sectors during an expansion, investors can potentially capitalize on the strong performance of businesses that benefit from increased economic activity and consumer spending.

Peak: Warning Signs and Market Behavior

The peak phase represents the highest point of economic activity before a downturn. It is a period where the economy operates at full capacity, but warning signs indicate that growth may soon slow or reverse:

- **Maximum Economic Output**: The economy reaches its maximum productive capacity, with high levels of production and consumption.

- **Inflation Pressures**: Rising demand for goods and services can lead to inflation as prices increase.
- **Tight Labor Markets**: Low unemployment rates can result in wage inflation as businesses compete for a limited pool of workers.

Key Indicators:
- **High Capacity Utilization**: Indicates that businesses are producing at near maximum capacity, which can lead to supply constraints and higher prices.
- **Rising Interest Rates**: Central banks may raise interest rates to control inflation, making borrowing more expensive and potentially slowing economic growth.
- **Inflation Rates**: Higher inflation rates can signal that the economy is overheating and may be due for a correction.

Sector Performance:

During the peak phase, certain sectors may start to underperform as the economy reaches its limits, while others may continue to provide stable returns. Here's a closer look at the sectors that tend to perform well during the peak phase:

- **Healthcare**: The healthcare sector is considered defensive because it provides essential services and products that are in demand regardless of economic conditions. Companies in pharmaceuticals, medical devices, and healthcare services often see steady revenues and profits during the peak phase, as healthcare spending remains consistent.
- **Utilities**: Similar to healthcare, the utilities sector is also defensive. Utilities provide essential services such as electricity, water, and natural gas, which are necessary for everyday life. The demand for these services remains stable even when economic growth slows, making utilities a safe haven for investors seeking stability

during the peak phase.
- **Consumer Staples**: This sector includes companies that produce essential goods such as food, beverages, and household products. Consumer staples are less sensitive to economic fluctuations because people still need to buy these products regardless of economic conditions. During the peak phase, when growth sectors may become overvalued, consumer staples can provide steady returns.

Investing in these defensive sectors during the peak phase can help mitigate risks associated with an impending economic slowdown and provide a buffer against market volatility.

Contraction: Identifying Downturns and Sector Impact

The contraction phase, or recession, involves a decline in economic activity. It is marked by reduced consumer and business spending, leading to slower growth and rising unemployment:

- **Declining GDP**: Economic output decreases as consumer and business spending slows down.
- **Rising Unemployment**: Job losses increase, leading to higher unemployment rates as businesses cut back on production and costs.
- **Reduced Consumer Spending**: Lower income and job insecurity result in decreased consumer spending, further slowing the economy.

Key Indicators:
- **Decreasing Industrial Production**: Reflects reduced manufacturing and business activity as demand declines.
- **Declining Retail Sales**: Lower consumer spending signals economic contraction and reduced confidence in the economy.
- **Rising Unemployment**: Increased job losses indicate economic distress and reduced household income.

Sector Performance:

During the contraction phase, certain sectors prove more resilient due to their essential nature and consistent demand. Here's a closer look at the sectors that tend to perform well during a contraction:

- **Consumer Staples**: Companies in this sector produce essential goods such as food, beverages, and household products. The demand for these products remains stable even when the economy is struggling, as people still need to buy groceries and other necessities. Consumer staples companies often see consistent revenue and profits during a contraction, making them attractive to investors seeking stability.
- **Utilities**: The utilities sector provides essential services such as electricity, water, and natural gas. The demand for these services does not fluctuate significantly with economic conditions, as people and businesses still require power and water. Utilities companies often have regulated revenue streams, which provide predictability and stability during economic downturns.
- **Healthcare**: The healthcare sector includes pharmaceuticals, medical devices, and healthcare services. The demand for healthcare remains strong regardless of economic conditions, as people continue to need medical care and medications. Healthcare companies can offer stability and growth opportunities even during a recession, as they provide essential services.

Focusing on these resilient sectors during a contraction can help protect an investment portfolio from the worst effects of an economic downturn and provide more stable returns.

Trough: Recovery Signals and Sector Opportunities

The trough phase marks the lowest point of the economic cycle, followed by recovery. During this phase, economic activity

stabilizes, and early signs of recovery begin to appear:
- **Stabilizing GDP**: Economic output stops declining and begins to stabilize, indicating the end of the contraction phase.
- **Early Signs of Recovery**: Indicators such as rising consumer confidence, increased business investments, and stabilizing employment suggest that the economy is beginning to recover.
- **High Unemployment**: Although unemployment may remain high, the rate of job losses slows, and job creation starts to pick up.

Key Indicators:
- **Stabilizing Industrial Production**: Indicates that the economy is no longer contracting.
- **Rising Consumer Confidence**: Reflects optimism about economic recovery.
- **Increased Business Investments**: Businesses start investing in anticipation of future growth.

Sector Performance:

During the trough phase, certain sectors tend to lead the recovery as economic conditions improve. Here's a closer look at the sectors that typically perform well during this phase:
- **Financials**: The financial sector often leads the recovery as banks, insurance companies, and other financial institutions benefit from improved economic conditions. As businesses and consumers gain confidence, demand for loans, mortgages, and other financial services increases. Additionally, rising interest rates can improve the profitability of banks, making the financial sector an attractive investment during the early stages of recovery.
- **Consumer Discretionary**: As the economy begins to recover, consumer confidence improves, and people

start spending more on non-essential goods and services. This includes sectors such as retail, automotive, and entertainment. Companies that offer discretionary products and services often see a boost in sales and profitability as consumers feel more secure about their financial future.

- **Industrials**: The industrials sector benefits from increased business activity and investments in infrastructure and capital goods. As businesses ramp up production and expand operations, demand for industrial products and services grows. Companies involved in construction, machinery manufacturing, and transportation often see improved performance during the recovery phase.
- **Technology**: The technology sector can also benefit during the recovery phase as businesses and consumers invest in new technologies to improve efficiency and productivity. Companies involved in software development, hardware production, and tech services often see increased demand as the economy starts to recover.

By focusing on these sectors during the trough phase, investors can potentially capitalize on the early stages of economic recovery and position their portfolios for future growth.

Indicators of Each Phase

Understanding the indicators that signal each phase of the economic cycle is crucial for effective sector rotation. These indicators can be classified into three categories: leading, lagging, and coincident.

Leading Indicators

Leading indicators signal future economic activity and can help predict the onset of economic phases:

- **Stock Market Performance**: Often rises before the

economy improves and falls before the economy declines. Investors anticipate economic conditions and adjust their portfolios accordingly, making the stock market a key leading indicator.

- **Manufacturing Activity**: Increases in manufacturing orders and production typically precede economic expansion. Rising demand for goods suggests that businesses are gearing up for future growth.
- **New Business Startups**: An increase in new businesses suggests optimism and potential economic growth. Entrepreneurs are more likely to start new ventures when they expect favorable economic conditions.

Lagging Indicators

Lagging indicators confirm trends and changes in the economy, typically after the fact:

- **Unemployment Rates**: Employment trends often lag behind economic shifts, increasing during contractions and decreasing during expansions. As businesses react to economic conditions, changes in employment levels take time to materialize.
- **Corporate Profits**: Profits reflect past economic performance and tend to lag behind economic changes. Higher profits indicate that businesses have successfully navigated recent economic conditions.
- **Interest Rates**: Central banks adjust interest rates in response to economic conditions, often after trends have been established. Higher interest rates may signal efforts to curb inflation, while lower rates indicate attempts to stimulate economic activity.

Coincident Indicators

Coincident indicators occur in real-time with economic activity, providing a snapshot of the current economic phase:

- **GDP**: Measures overall economic output and reflects current economic conditions. An increase in GDP

indicates economic growth, while a decrease suggests contraction.
- **Employment Levels**: Current employment data indicates the health of the labor market. Higher employment levels reflect a robust economy, while lower levels indicate economic challenges.
- **Income Levels**: Household income reflects current economic stability and consumer spending power. Higher incomes suggest a strong economy, while lower incomes indicate potential economic difficulties.

Key Economic Metrics

Key metrics provide valuable insights into the economic cycle:
- **GDP**: A primary measure of economic activity that indicates the overall health of the economy.
- **Unemployment**: Reflects the health of the labor market and economic conditions. Lower unemployment rates indicate economic growth, while higher rates suggest contraction.
- **Inflation**: Indicates price stability and purchasing power. Moderate inflation is a sign of economic growth, while high inflation can signal overheating, and deflation suggests economic weakness.

Real-World Examples and Historical Data

Real-world examples and historical data help illustrate the concepts of economic cycles and their impact on sector performance. By analyzing past economic cycles, investors can gain valuable insights into how different sectors perform during various phases and apply these lessons to future investment strategies.

Historical Examples of Economic Cycles

Analyzing historical economic cycles provides valuable insights into sector performance and investment strategies. By examining past events, investors can better understand how different sectors respond to economic changes and identify patterns that may inform future decisions.

The Great Depression (1929-1939)

The Great Depression was one of the most severe economic downturns in history, characterized by massive declines in GDP, skyrocketing unemployment, and deflationary pressures.

Economic Indicators:

- **GDP**: Fell by nearly 30% during the worst years of the Depression.
- **Unemployment**: Peaked at around 25%, with millions of Americans losing their jobs.
- **Deflation**: Prices for goods and services dropped significantly, exacerbating economic challenges.

Sector Performance:

- **Utilities**: Utilities companies, which provide essential services like electricity and water, were more resilient during the Great Depression. Despite the economic downturn, people still needed access to these basic services, making utilities a relatively stable investment.
- **Consumer Staples**: Companies producing essential goods, such as food and household products, also fared better. Demand for these products remained steady as consumers continued to purchase necessities.

Lessons Learned:

- **Diversification**: The importance of diversification and having exposure to defensive sectors became evident during the Great Depression. Investors who allocated a portion of their portfolios to utilities and consumer staples were better able to weather the storm.
- **Government Intervention**: The role of government intervention in stabilizing the economy was highlighted, leading to the creation of programs like the New Deal, which aimed to stimulate economic growth and provide relief to those affected by the downturn.

Post-WWII Boom (1945-1960s)

The post-WWII period was marked by sustained economic growth, rising consumer spending, and low unemployment, creating a favorable environment for many sectors.

Economic Indicators:

- **GDP**: Grew consistently as the economy expanded and industrial production increased.
- **Consumer Spending**: Rose significantly as households enjoyed higher incomes and greater access to credit.
- **Unemployment**: Remained low, reflecting strong job creation and economic stability.

Sector Performance:

- **Consumer Discretionary**: The consumer discretionary sector thrived as Americans enjoyed newfound prosperity and spent more on luxury items, automobiles, and entertainment. Companies in retail, automotive, and leisure industries saw substantial growth.
- **Industrials**: The industrials sector benefited from increased investments in infrastructure and manufacturing. Companies involved in construction, machinery production, and transportation experienced robust demand as the economy expanded.

Lessons Learned:

- **Capitalizing on Growth**: Investors who recognized the potential for sustained economic growth and allocated their portfolios accordingly reaped significant rewards. Focusing on sectors poised to benefit from increased consumer spending and industrial activity proved to be a successful strategy.
- **Innovation and Expansion**: The importance of innovation and expansion during periods of economic growth was highlighted. Companies that invested in

new technologies and expanded their operations were well-positioned to capitalize on the post-WWII boom.

Dot-com Bubble (Late 1990s-Early 2000s)

The dot-com bubble was characterized by rapid expansion and significant overvaluation of technology companies, followed by a sharp contraction and market correction.

Economic Indicators:

- **GDP**: Experienced rapid growth during the boom, driven by investments in technology and internet-based businesses.
- **Stock Market**: The NASDAQ index, heavily weighted with technology stocks, soared to unprecedented levels before crashing.
- **Unemployment**: Initially low, but increased as the bubble burst and companies laid off workers.

Sector Performance:

- **Technology**: The technology sector saw extraordinary gains during the boom, with many internet-based companies experiencing exponential growth. However, when the bubble burst, the sector suffered severe losses as valuations plummeted and many companies went bankrupt.
- **Telecom**: Similar to technology, the telecom sector experienced rapid expansion and overvaluation, followed by a significant downturn when the bubble burst.
- **Defensive Sectors**: During the market correction, defensive sectors such as healthcare, utilities, and consumer staples provided stability and performed relatively well as investors sought safer investments.

Lessons Learned:

- **Valuation Risks**: The risks associated with overvaluation and the importance of conducting

thorough fundamental analysis were underscored by the dot-com bubble. Investors learned the dangers of speculative investments and the need for a balanced portfolio.
- **Sector Rotation**: The value of sector rotation became evident as investors who shifted their focus from overvalued technology stocks to defensive sectors were better able to protect their portfolios during the downturn.

Global Financial Crisis (2007-2009)

The global financial crisis was a severe economic downturn triggered by the collapse of the housing market and widespread financial instability.

Economic Indicators:
- **GDP**: Contracted sharply as the housing market collapsed and financial institutions faced significant losses.
- **Unemployment**: Rose dramatically, with millions of people losing their jobs.
- **Housing Market**: Experienced a severe downturn, with home prices plummeting and foreclosures rising.

Sector Performance:
- **Financials**: The financial sector suffered the most during the crisis, with many banks and financial institutions facing insolvency or requiring government bailouts. The collapse of Lehman Brothers and other major financial firms highlighted the sector's vulnerability.
- **Real Estate**: The real estate sector also experienced severe losses as home prices fell and foreclosures increased. Companies involved in real estate development, construction, and mortgage lending faced significant challenges.
- **Consumer Staples and Healthcare**: These defensive

sectors proved more resilient during the crisis. Companies providing essential goods and services, such as food, beverages, and healthcare, continued to perform relatively well as demand for their products remained steady.

Lessons Learned:

- **Risk Management**: The importance of risk management and diversification was reinforced by the global financial crisis. Investors who diversified their portfolios and included defensive sectors were better able to weather the downturn.
- **Government Intervention**: The role of government intervention in stabilizing the economy was highlighted once again, with measures such as the Troubled Asset Relief Program (TARP) and quantitative easing helping to mitigate the impact of the crisis.

By understanding these historical cycles and their impact on sector performance, investors can gain valuable insights into how to navigate future economic phases and effectively implement sector rotation strategies.

CHAPTER 2: SECTOR CLASSIFICATION

To implement effective sector rotation strategies, it's crucial to understand how sectors are classified and the unique characteristics that define each one. This chapter covers the basics of sector classification, the major sectors in the economy, and the tools used to categorize them.

Defining Sectors and Industries

Understanding the difference between sectors and industries is essential for effective investment strategy.

- **Sectors**: Broad segments of the economy, composed of multiple industries. For example, the Technology sector includes industries such as software, hardware, and IT services.
- **Industries**: More specific groups of companies within a sector that have similar business activities. For example, within the Technology sector, the semiconductor industry focuses specifically on companies that manufacture semiconductor products.

This hierarchical structure helps investors analyze and compare companies more efficiently by grouping them based on shared economic characteristics.

Major Sectors in the Economy

Each sector of the economy plays a distinct role and responds differently to economic cycles. Here is an overview of key sectors and their primary drivers:

1. **Technology**
   - **Characteristics**: Innovation-driven, rapid growth potential, high R&D investment.
   - **Primary Drivers**: Technological advancements, consumer demand for new products, business investment in IT infrastructure.

The Technology sector is at the forefront of innovation and transformation, encompassing companies that develop software, manufacture hardware, and provide IT services. This sector is characterized by rapid growth potential due to continuous advancements in technology and the high levels of research and development (R&D) investment required. Companies in this sector often experience substantial growth as they introduce new products and services that revolutionize industries.

Performance and Drivers:
   - **Technological Advancements**: Innovations such as artificial intelligence, cloud computing, and 5G technology drive growth in this sector.
   - **Consumer Demand**: High consumer demand for the latest gadgets, software, and digital services propels the sector forward.
   - **Business Investment**: Companies invest heavily in IT infrastructure to improve efficiency, productivity, and competitive advantage.
   - **Economic Sensitivity**: While generally resilient, the sector can be sensitive to economic downturns due to its reliance on business investment and

consumer spending.

2. **Healthcare**
    - **Characteristics**: Essential services, stable demand, significant regulatory oversight.
    - **Primary Drivers**: Aging population, medical innovations, healthcare policy changes.

The Healthcare sector includes companies that provide medical services, manufacture medical equipment, and develop pharmaceuticals. This sector is essential and less sensitive to economic cycles due to the consistent demand for healthcare services. Innovations in medical technology and treatments continuously drive growth, and an aging population increases the demand for healthcare services.

Performance and Drivers:
    - **Aging Population**: As the population ages, the demand for healthcare services and products increases.
    - **Medical Innovations**: Advances in medical technology and pharmaceuticals contribute to sector growth.
    - **Healthcare Policies**: Regulatory changes and healthcare reforms can impact sector performance.
    - **Economic Sensitivity**: The sector is generally defensive, maintaining stable demand during economic downturns.

3. **Financials**
    - **Characteristics**: Includes banks, insurance companies, and investment firms; sensitive to interest rates.
    - **Primary Drivers**: Economic growth, interest rate changes, financial market performance.

The Financials sector comprises banks, insurance companies, investment firms, and real estate companies.

This sector is closely tied to the overall economy and is sensitive to interest rate changes. Economic growth boosts demand for financial services, while rising interest rates can enhance profitability for banks through higher net interest margins.

Performance and Drivers:

- **Economic Growth**: A growing economy increases demand for banking, insurance, and investment services.
- **Interest Rates**: Changes in interest rates significantly impact the profitability of financial institutions.
- **Financial Market Performance**: Market conditions and investor sentiment influence the performance of financial services firms.
- **Economic Sensitivity**: Highly sensitive to economic conditions, with performance closely tied to economic cycles.

4. **Consumer Discretionary**
    - **Characteristics**: Non-essential goods and services, high sensitivity to economic cycles.
    - **Primary Drivers**: Consumer confidence, disposable income levels, economic growth.

The Consumer Discretionary sector includes companies that provide non-essential goods and services such as retail, automotive, and entertainment. This sector is highly sensitive to economic cycles, performing well during periods of economic growth when consumer confidence and disposable income are high.

Performance and Drivers:

- **Consumer Confidence**: High consumer confidence drives spending on non-essential items.
- **Disposable Income**: Increases in disposable income

lead to higher spending on discretionary goods and services.
- **Economic Growth**: Economic expansion boosts demand for luxury items, travel, and entertainment.
- **Economic Sensitivity**: Highly sensitive to economic downturns, with reduced consumer spending impacting sector performance.

5. **Consumer Staples**
   - **Characteristics**: Essential goods and services, low sensitivity to economic cycles.
   - **Primary Drivers**: Population growth, consistent demand, economic stability.

The Consumer Staples sector includes companies that produce essential goods such as food, beverages, and household products. This sector is less sensitive to economic cycles as the demand for these products remains consistent regardless of economic conditions.

Performance and Drivers:
- **Population Growth**: A growing population increases demand for essential goods.
- **Consistent Demand**: Steady demand for essential products ensures stable revenues for companies in this sector.
- **Economic Stability**: Performs well during economic downturns as consumers prioritize essential purchases.
- **Economic Sensitivity**: Generally defensive, providing stability during economic uncertainty.

6. **Industrials**
   - **Characteristics**: Involves manufacturing and infrastructure; capital-intensive.
   - **Primary Drivers**: Business investment,

government infrastructure spending, economic growth.

The Industrials sector includes companies involved in manufacturing, construction, and transportation. This sector is capital-intensive and benefits from business investment and government spending on infrastructure projects. Economic growth stimulates demand for industrial goods and services.

Performance and Drivers:

- **Business Investment**: Increases in business capital expenditures drive demand for industrial products.
- **Government Spending**: Infrastructure projects funded by governments boost sector performance.
- **Economic Growth**: Economic expansion leads to higher demand for manufactured goods and transportation services.
- **Economic Sensitivity**: Sensitive to economic cycles, with performance closely tied to economic activity levels.

7. **Energy**
    - **Characteristics**: Involves oil, gas, and renewable energy; highly volatile.
    - **Primary Drivers**: Energy prices, geopolitical events, technological advancements in energy.

The Energy sector includes companies involved in the production and distribution of oil, gas, and renewable energy. This sector is highly volatile, influenced by energy prices, geopolitical events, and technological advancements in energy production and distribution.

Performance and Drivers:

- **Energy Prices**: Fluctuations in oil and gas prices significantly impact sector profitability.
- **Geopolitical Events**: Political instability and

conflicts in key energy-producing regions affect supply and prices.
- **Technological Advancements**: Innovations in energy production, such as fracking and renewable energy technologies, drive sector evolution.
- **Economic Sensitivity**: Highly volatile, with performance impacted by both economic cycles and external factors.

8. **Utilities**
   - **Characteristics**: Essential services like electricity and water; regulated industry.
   - **Primary Drivers**: Population growth, regulatory changes, infrastructure investments.

The Utilities sector provides essential services such as electricity, water, and natural gas. This sector is highly regulated, ensuring stable demand and predictable revenue streams. Population growth and infrastructure investments drive demand for utility services.

Performance and Drivers:
- **Population Growth**: Increases in population lead to higher demand for utility services.
- **Regulatory Changes**: Government regulations and policies impact sector operations and profitability.
- **Infrastructure Investments**: Investments in utility infrastructure enhance service delivery and sector performance.
- **Economic Sensitivity**: Generally defensive, providing stability during economic downturns due to consistent demand for essential services.

9. **Materials**
   - **Characteristics**: Involves mining, chemicals, and forestry; linked to commodity prices.

- **Primary Drivers**: Economic growth, industrial production, commodity price fluctuations.

The Materials sector includes companies involved in the extraction and processing of raw materials such as metals, chemicals, and forestry products. This sector is closely linked to commodity prices and industrial production, with demand driven by economic growth and infrastructure projects.

Performance and Drivers:

- **Economic Growth**: Higher economic activity boosts demand for raw materials.
- **Industrial Production**: Increases in manufacturing and construction drive demand for materials.
- **Commodity Prices**: Fluctuations in prices of metals, chemicals, and other materials impact sector profitability.
- **Economic Sensitivity**: Sensitive to economic cycles, with performance linked to industrial demand and commodity price trends.

10. **Real Estate**

- **Characteristics**: Includes residential, commercial, and industrial properties; interest rate sensitive.
- **Primary Drivers**: Interest rates, economic growth, housing market trends.

The Real Estate sector encompasses companies involved in the development, ownership, and management of residential, commercial, and industrial properties. This sector is sensitive to interest rates, as borrowing costs influence property investments and valuations.

Performance and Drivers:

- **Interest Rates**: Changes in interest rates affect mortgage rates, property values, and real estate

investment.
- **Economic Growth**: Economic expansion drives demand for residential and commercial properties.
- **Housing Market Trends**: Housing demand, supply dynamics, and property prices influence sector performance.
- **Economic Sensitivity**: Interest rate sensitive, with performance impacted by borrowing costs and economic conditions.

By understanding the characteristics and primary drivers of each sector, investors can make informed decisions about sector rotation strategies and optimize their investment portfolios.

Tools for Sector Classification

Accurate classification of sectors and industries is crucial for analyzing and comparing companies. Several classification systems are widely used by investors and analysts:

1. **GICS (Global Industry Classification Standard)**
   - **Developed by**: MSCI and S&P Dow Jones Indices.
   - **Structure**: Four levels—sectors, industry groups, industries, and sub-industries.
   - **Usage**: Widely adopted by major financial institutions and used for benchmarking and index construction.

2. **ICB (Industry Classification Benchmark)**
   - **Developed by**: FTSE Russell.
   - **Structure**: Four levels—industries, supersectors, sectors, and subsectors.
   - **Usage**: Used primarily in European and Asian markets, applied for index composition and sector analysis.

3. **NAICS (North American Industry Classification System)**

- **Developed by**: Governments of the U.S., Canada, and Mexico.
- **Structure**: Hierarchical classification with 20 sectors divided into subsectors, industry groups, industries, and U.S. industries.
- **Usage**: Used for government statistics, economic analysis, and business data reporting.

4. **SIC (Standard Industrial Classification)**
   - **Developed by**: U.S. government.
   - **Structure**: Four-digit codes classifying industries.
   - **Usage**: Historical classification system, still used for certain regulatory and administrative purposes.

Comparing these classification systems can help investors choose the most appropriate tool for their analysis needs. GICS and ICB are commonly used for investment analysis and portfolio construction, while NAICS and SIC are more prevalent in economic and business research.

Importance of Accurate Classification

Accurate sector classification is crucial for several reasons:

- **Performance Benchmarking**: Comparing a company's performance against its sector helps identify strengths and weaknesses relative to peers.
- **Sector Allocation**: Understanding sector classifications aids in constructing a diversified portfolio, ensuring exposure to different parts of the economy.
- **Economic Analysis**: Sector classification provides insights into how different parts of the economy contribute to overall growth and respond to economic cycles.
- **Risk Management**: Identifying sector-specific risks and

opportunities helps in making informed investment decisions and managing portfolio risk.

By understanding sector classification and the unique characteristics of each sector, investors can better implement sector rotation strategies and optimize their investment portfolios.

CHAPTER 3: THE THEORY BEHIND SECTOR ROTATION

Sector rotation is grounded in the understanding that different sectors of the economy perform differently during various phases of the economic cycle. By strategically shifting investments among sectors, investors can potentially enhance returns and reduce risks. This chapter delves into the theory behind sector rotation, the correlation between economic cycles and sector performance, historical performance data, and the rationale for rotating sectors.

Economic Cycle and Sector Performance Correlation

Economic cycles have a profound impact on sector performance. Each phase of the economic cycle—expansion, peak, contraction, and trough—affects sectors differently. Understanding these correlations helps investors make informed decisions about which sectors to invest in and when.

Expansion Phase

During the expansion phase, the economy experiences growth characterized by rising GDP, increasing employment, and higher consumer and business spending. Key sectors that typically perform well during this phase include:

- **Technology**: Innovation and increased business investment in technology drive growth.
- **Consumer Discretionary**: Higher disposable income leads to increased spending on non-essential goods and services.
- **Industrials**: Business expansion and infrastructure development boost demand for industrial goods and services.

Historical data supports these correlations. For instance, during the economic expansion from 2003 to 2007, the Technology sector experienced significant growth, driven by advancements in internet technology and increased IT spending by businesses.

Peak Phase

The peak phase marks the highest point of economic activity before a downturn. During this phase, inflationary pressures build, and economic growth slows. Defensive sectors often outperform as investors seek stability:

- **Healthcare**: Provides essential services that remain in demand regardless of economic conditions.
- **Utilities**: Offers essential services such as electricity and water, with stable demand.
- **Consumer Staples**: Produces essential goods like food and beverages, maintaining steady demand.

For example, in the period leading up to the 2008 financial crisis, defensive sectors like Healthcare and Consumer Staples outperformed as economic growth slowed and investors sought safer investments.

Contraction Phase

The contraction phase, or recession, involves declining economic activity, rising unemployment, and reduced consumer and business spending. Defensive sectors continue to perform well, while cyclical sectors suffer:

- **Consumer Staples**: Essential goods maintain demand.
- **Utilities**: Stable demand for essential services.
- **Healthcare**: Consistent need for medical services and products.

During the 2008-2009 financial crisis, sectors like Financials and Industrials suffered significant losses, while Consumer Staples and Healthcare demonstrated resilience.

Trough Phase

The trough phase represents the lowest point of economic activity, followed by recovery. Early cyclical sectors typically lead the recovery as economic conditions begin to improve:

- **Financials**: Benefit from improved credit conditions and increased lending.
- **Consumer Discretionary**: Higher consumer confidence and spending boost demand.
- **Industrials**: Increased business investment and infrastructure development drive growth.

For instance, following the 2009 recession, the Financials and Consumer Discretionary sectors led the recovery as economic conditions stabilized and confidence returned.

Historical Performance of Sectors in Different Economic Phases

Analyzing historical performance data provides valuable insights into how sectors respond to different economic phases. By examining past economic cycles, investors can identify patterns and make informed decisions about sector rotation strategies.

Expansion Examples

- **Dot-com Boom (1990s)**: The Technology sector experienced explosive growth due to the rise of the internet and e-commerce.
- **Pre-2008 Financial Crisis (2003-2007)**: The Industrials and Consumer Discretionary sectors thrived as economic conditions improved and consumer spending increased.

Peak Examples
- **Late 1990s**: Defensive sectors like Healthcare and Utilities outperformed as the economy reached its peak and inflationary pressures built.
- **Pre-2008 Financial Crisis**: Investors shifted to Consumer Staples and Utilities as economic growth slowed and risks increased.

Contraction Examples
- **2008-2009 Financial Crisis**: The Financials and Industrials sectors suffered severe losses, while Consumer Staples and Healthcare remained stable.
- **Early 2000s Recession**: Technology and Telecom sectors faced significant declines, while Utilities and Consumer Staples provided stability.

Trough Examples
- **Post-2009 Recovery**: Financials and Consumer Discretionary sectors led the recovery as economic conditions improved.
- **Post-1980s Recession**: Early cyclical sectors like Industrials and Financials outperformed during the recovery phase.

The Rationale for Rotating Sectors

Sector rotation strategies are based on the premise that different sectors perform differently during various phases of the economic cycle. By anticipating economic shifts and rotating investments accordingly, investors can potentially optimize their portfolio performance.

Key Benefits of Sector Rotation:

- **Enhanced Returns**: By investing in sectors that are expected to outperform during specific economic phases, investors can potentially achieve higher returns.
- **Risk Reduction**: Rotating investments into defensive sectors during economic downturns can help mitigate

losses and protect the portfolio.
- **Diversification**: Sector rotation provides diversification across different parts of the economy, reducing exposure to sector-specific risks.

Challenges of Sector Rotation:
- **Timing**: Accurately predicting economic phases and market conditions is challenging and requires careful analysis and monitoring of economic indicators.
- **Transaction Costs**: Frequent trading to rotate sectors can incur higher transaction costs, impacting overall returns.
- **Market Volatility**: Unexpected market events and volatility can disrupt sector rotation strategies, leading to potential losses.

Implementing Sector Rotation:
- **Economic Analysis**: Monitor key economic indicators such as GDP growth, inflation rates, employment data, and consumer confidence to identify economic phases.
- **Sector Analysis**: Evaluate sector performance, industry trends, and company fundamentals to determine the most promising sectors for each phase.
- **Regular Review**: Continuously review and adjust the portfolio to reflect changing economic conditions and market dynamics.

By understanding the theory behind sector rotation and analyzing historical performance data, investors can make informed decisions and effectively implement sector rotation strategies to enhance returns and manage risks.

CHAPTER 4: IMPLEMENTING SECTOR ROTATION STRATEGIES

Implementing sector rotation strategies requires a thorough understanding of economic cycles, sector performance, and the use of analytical tools. This chapter will guide you through the process of identifying economic phases, selecting sectors to invest in during each phase, and timing and frequency of rotations.

Identifying Economic Cycle Phases

Accurately identifying the current phase of the economic cycle is crucial for effective sector rotation. This involves monitoring a variety of economic indicators and understanding their implications.

Key Economic Indicators to Monitor

Economic indicators provide valuable insights into the current state of the economy and help investors anticipate changes in

economic phases. Here are the key indicators to monitor:
- **GDP Growth**
- **Employment Data**
- **Inflation Rates**
- **Consumer Confidence**
- **Interest Rates**

GDP Growth

Gross Domestic Product (GDP) measures the total value of goods and services produced within a country over a specific period. It is one of the most comprehensive indicators of economic activity and health.

- **Positive GDP Growth**: Indicates economic expansion, characterized by increased production, higher consumer spending, and business investments. Sustained positive GDP growth suggests the economy is in the expansion phase.
- **Negative GDP Growth**: Signifies economic contraction, where production and consumer spending decrease. Persistent negative GDP growth can indicate a recession or economic downturn.

How to Monitor:
- **Quarterly GDP Reports**: Released by national statistical agencies, these reports provide detailed insights into the economy's performance.
- **Annual GDP Growth Rates**: Offer a broader perspective on long-term economic trends.

Impact on Sectors:
- During periods of strong GDP growth, sectors such as Technology, Consumer Discretionary, and Industrials typically perform well as consumer and business spending increases.
- In contrast, during periods of negative GDP growth, defensive sectors like Consumer Staples, Utilities, and

Healthcare tend to outperform as they provide essential goods and services that remain in demand.

Employment Data

Employment data includes various metrics that reflect the health of the labor market and overall economic activity.

- **Employment Rates**: The percentage of the labor force that is employed. Higher employment rates suggest economic strength and expansion.
- **Unemployment Rates**: The percentage of the labor force that is unemployed and actively seeking work. Rising unemployment rates indicate economic contraction and potential recession.
- **Job Creation Numbers**: The number of new jobs created within a specific period. Increasing job creation signals economic growth and expansion.

How to Monitor:

- **Monthly Employment Reports**: Released by government agencies, these reports provide data on employment rates, unemployment rates, and job creation.
- **Labor Force Participation Rate**: Measures the active portion of the labor force, providing additional context to employment and unemployment data.

Impact on Sectors:

- Rising employment and job creation boost consumer confidence and spending, benefiting sectors such as Consumer Discretionary and Financials.
- Conversely, increasing unemployment rates may lead to reduced consumer spending, favoring defensive sectors like Consumer Staples and Utilities.

Inflation Rates

Inflation measures the rate at which the general price level of goods and services rises, eroding purchasing power. It is a critical indicator of economic stability and central bank policies.

- **High Inflation**: Indicates increasing prices and potentially overheating economic conditions. Central banks may raise interest rates to control inflation, signaling a peak phase.
- **Low or Negative Inflation**: Suggests weak demand and potential economic stagnation or contraction. Central banks may lower interest rates to stimulate economic activity.

How to Monitor:

- **Consumer Price Index (CPI)**: Measures the average change in prices paid by consumers for a basket of goods and services. It is a primary indicator of inflation.
- **Producer Price Index (PPI)**: Measures the average change in prices received by domestic producers for their output. It provides insights into future consumer price trends.

Impact on Sectors:

- High inflation can negatively impact sectors with high input costs, such as Industrials and Consumer Discretionary, as higher prices may reduce consumer spending and business investments.
- Sectors like Utilities and Consumer Staples, which provide essential goods and services, may perform better during periods of high inflation as demand for their products remains stable.

Consumer Confidence

Consumer confidence measures how optimistic consumers are about the economy and their financial situation. It is a leading indicator of consumer spending and economic activity.

- **High Consumer Confidence**: Indicates that consumers are optimistic about the economy and are more likely to increase spending, driving economic growth.

- **Low Consumer Confidence**: Suggests that consumers are pessimistic about the economy, leading to reduced spending and potential economic contraction.

How to Monitor:
- **Consumer Confidence Index (CCI)**: A widely used measure of consumer sentiment, reflecting consumers' expectations regarding the economy.
- **Surveys and Reports**: Various organizations conduct surveys to gauge consumer confidence and spending intentions.

Impact on Sectors:
- High consumer confidence boosts sectors reliant on consumer spending, such as Consumer Discretionary and Financials.
- Low consumer confidence may favor defensive sectors like Consumer Staples and Healthcare, as consumers focus on essential goods and services.

Interest Rates

Interest rates set by central banks influence borrowing costs, consumer spending, and business investments. They are a crucial tool for managing economic stability and growth.

- **Rising Interest Rates**: Central banks increase rates to control inflation and cool down an overheating economy. This often signals an approaching peak phase.
- **Falling Interest Rates**: Central banks lower rates to stimulate economic activity during periods of low growth or recession, indicating a trough or early expansion phase.

How to Monitor:
- **Central Bank Announcements**: Regular updates from central banks on interest rate decisions and economic outlook.
- **Bond Yields**: The yield curve, particularly the difference

between short-term and long-term bond yields, provides insights into market expectations for future interest rates and economic activity.

Impact on Sectors:

- Rising interest rates can negatively impact sectors such as Real Estate and Financials, as higher borrowing costs reduce consumer and business spending.
- Falling interest rates benefit sectors like Financials and Consumer Discretionary, as lower borrowing costs stimulate lending and spending.

Practical Steps for Monitoring Indicators

1. **Set Up Alerts**: Use financial news services and platforms to set up alerts for key economic data releases and central bank announcements.
2. **Regularly Review Economic Reports**: Schedule time to review monthly, quarterly, and annual reports on GDP, employment, inflation, and consumer confidence.
3. **Follow Expert Analysis**: Read reports and analysis from economists and financial experts to gain insights into economic trends and implications for sector performance.
4. **Utilize Financial Tools**: Leverage tools and platforms that provide real-time data and economic indicators, such as Bloomberg, Reuters, and government websites.

Choosing Sectors to Invest in During Each Phase

Once the current economic phase is identified, the next step is to select sectors that are likely to perform well during that phase. Here's a detailed guide for each phase:

Expansion Phase:

- **Technology**: Invest in companies that are innovating and expanding, such as those in software, hardware, and IT services.
- **Consumer Discretionary**: Focus on retail, automotive,

and entertainment companies that benefit from increased consumer spending.
- **Industrials**: Consider companies involved in construction, manufacturing, and transportation that grow with increased business investments.

Sector Analysis:
- **Technology**: Companies like Apple, Microsoft, and Alphabet often lead in innovation and growth during expansions due to increased consumer and business spending on technology.
- **Consumer Discretionary**: Retailers like Amazon and automakers like Tesla see heightened demand as consumers feel confident and spend more.
- **Industrials**: Companies like Caterpillar and Boeing benefit from increased infrastructure projects and business investments.

Peak Phase:
- **Healthcare**: Invest in pharmaceutical, biotechnology, and medical device companies that provide essential services.
- **Utilities**: Focus on electricity, water, and natural gas providers that offer stability and consistent returns.
- **Consumer Staples**: Choose companies producing essential goods like food, beverages, and household products.

Sector Analysis:
- **Healthcare**: Companies like Johnson & Johnson and Pfizer remain in demand as they provide essential health services and products.
- **Utilities**: Providers like Duke Energy and Southern Company offer stable returns due to consistent demand for essential services.
- **Consumer Staples**: Companies like Procter & Gamble

and Coca-Cola continue to perform well as they offer products that remain in demand regardless of economic conditions.

Contraction Phase:
- **Consumer Staples**: Continue to invest in companies providing essential goods, as demand remains stable.
- **Utilities**: Maintain investments in essential service providers for their stable revenues.
- **Healthcare**: Focus on companies providing medical services and products, as demand is less sensitive to economic conditions.

Sector Analysis:
- **Consumer Staples**: Companies like Unilever and Nestlé provide essential products that consumers continue to buy during economic downturns.
- **Utilities**: Companies like NextEra Energy and American Electric Power offer stable revenue streams due to the necessity of their services.
- **Healthcare**: Firms like Medtronic and Gilead Sciences continue to see demand for their products and services, making them resilient during recessions.

Trough Phase:
- **Financials**: Invest in banks, insurance companies, and investment firms that benefit from improved economic conditions and increased lending.
- **Consumer Discretionary**: Look for companies that are poised to benefit from rising consumer confidence and spending.
- **Industrials**: Consider companies involved in infrastructure development and manufacturing, as they often lead the recovery.

Sector Analysis:
- **Financials**: Banks like JPMorgan Chase and Goldman

Sachs benefit from increased lending activity and improved economic conditions.

- **Consumer Discretionary**: Companies like Starbucks and Nike see a rebound in consumer spending as confidence returns.
- **Industrials**: Firms like General Electric and 3M benefit from increased infrastructure projects and business investments as the economy recovers.

Timing and Frequency of Rotations

Effective sector rotation requires careful timing and consideration of how frequently to adjust the portfolio.

Strategic vs. Tactical Sector Rotation:

- **Strategic Rotation**: Involves long-term investment decisions based on broad economic trends. Investors may hold positions for several months to years, adjusting their portfolios as major economic phases change.
- **Tactical Rotation**: Involves shorter-term adjustments based on more frequent economic indicators and market trends. Investors may rotate sectors on a monthly or quarterly basis to capitalize on shorter-term opportunities.

Balancing Short-Term Gains with Long-Term Goals:

- **Long-Term Stability**: Focus on sectors with strong fundamentals and growth prospects over the economic cycle. This approach helps in building a resilient portfolio.
- **Short-Term Opportunities**: Take advantage of market fluctuations and short-term trends by tactically rotating sectors. This requires more active management and frequent portfolio reviews.

Considerations for Effective Timing:

- **Economic Indicator Analysis**: Regularly review key

economic indicators to anticipate phase changes and adjust the portfolio accordingly.

- **Market Sentiment**: Monitor investor sentiment and market trends to identify potential turning points and opportunities.
- **Technical Analysis**: Use technical analysis tools such as moving averages, relative strength index (RSI), and support/resistance levels to time sector rotations.

Practical Steps for Sector Rotation:

1. **Set Clear Objectives**: Define your investment goals, risk tolerance, and time horizon.
2. **Develop a Watchlist**: Identify sectors and companies that align with your strategy and economic outlook.
3. **Monitor Indicators**: Regularly review economic indicators and market conditions to identify phase changes.
4. **Make Informed Decisions**: Use a combination of fundamental and technical analysis to decide when to rotate sectors.
5. **Review and Adjust**: Continuously review the portfolio and make adjustments as economic conditions and market trends evolve.

By carefully timing sector rotations and selecting the right sectors for each economic phase, investors can enhance returns and manage risks more effectively.

CHAPTER 5: ANALYTICAL TOOLS AND INDICATORS

To implement sector rotation strategies effectively, investors need to use a variety of analytical tools and indicators. These tools help in identifying economic phases, assessing sector performance, and making informed investment decisions. This chapter explores key economic indicators, technical analysis tools, and fundamental analysis techniques for evaluating sectors.

Key Economic Indicators to Monitor

Economic indicators provide valuable insights into the state of the economy and help investors anticipate changes in economic phases. Monitoring these indicators is crucial for making informed sector rotation decisions.

1. Leading Indicators

Leading indicators signal future economic activity and help predict the onset of economic phases. Key leading indicators include:

- **Stock Market Performance**: The stock market often rises before the economy improves and falls before the economy declines. It reflects investor sentiment and expectations about future economic conditions.
- **Manufacturing Activity**: Increases in manufacturing orders and production typically precede economic expansion. The Purchasing Managers' Index (PMI) is a widely watched indicator that provides insights into manufacturing activity.
- **New Business Startups**: An increase in new business formations suggests optimism and potential economic growth.

How to Monitor:
- **Stock Indices**: Monitor major stock indices such as the S&P 500, NASDAQ, and Dow Jones Industrial Average.
- **PMI Reports**: Published monthly by organizations such as the Institute for Supply Management (ISM) and IHS Markit.
- **Business Formation Data**: Available from government agencies and business registries.

Impact on Sectors:
- An improving stock market and rising PMI indicate potential economic expansion, benefiting sectors like Technology, Consumer Discretionary, and Industrials.

2. Lagging Indicators

Lagging indicators confirm trends and changes in the economy, typically after the fact. Key lagging indicators include:
- **Unemployment Rates**: Employment trends often lag behind economic shifts, increasing during contractions and decreasing during expansions.
- **Corporate Profits**: Profits reflect past economic performance and tend to lag behind economic changes.
- **Interest Rates**: Central banks adjust interest rates in

response to economic conditions, often after trends have been established.

How to Monitor:
- **Monthly Employment Reports**: Released by government agencies, providing data on unemployment rates and job creation.
- **Corporate Earnings Reports**: Published quarterly by publicly traded companies.
- **Central Bank Announcements**: Regular updates on interest rate decisions and economic outlook from institutions like the Federal Reserve and European Central Bank.

Impact on Sectors:
- Rising unemployment and declining corporate profits confirm economic contraction, favoring defensive sectors like Consumer Staples, Utilities, and Healthcare.

3. Coincident Indicators

Coincident indicators occur in real-time with economic activity, providing a snapshot of the current economic phase. Key coincident indicators include:

- **GDP**: Measures overall economic output and reflects current economic conditions.
- **Employment Levels**: Current employment data indicates the health of the labor market.
- **Income Levels**: Household income reflects current economic stability and consumer spending power.

How to Monitor:
- **Quarterly GDP Reports**: Provide detailed insights into the economy's performance.
- **Employment Data**: Monthly reports from government agencies.
- **Income and Wage Reports**: Published by government

statistical agencies.

Impact on Sectors:
- Positive GDP growth and rising employment levels indicate economic expansion, benefiting sectors like Technology, Consumer Discretionary, and Industrials.

Technical Analysis Tools

Technical analysis involves analyzing historical price and volume data to predict future market movements. It helps investors identify trends, entry and exit points, and potential reversals.

1. Moving Averages

Moving averages smooth out price data to identify trends and potential support/resistance levels.

- **Simple Moving Average (SMA)**: The average price over a specific period. Common periods include 50-day and 200-day SMAs.
- **Exponential Moving Average (EMA)**: Gives more weight to recent prices, making it more responsive to current market conditions.

How to Use:
- **Trend Identification**: Rising moving averages indicate an uptrend, while falling moving averages indicate a downtrend. For example, a 50-day moving average trending above a 200-day moving average generally signifies an uptrend.
- **Crossovers**: When a short-term moving average crosses above a long-term moving average (golden cross), it signals a potential buy. Conversely, when it crosses below (death cross), it signals a potential sell.

Impact on Sectors:
- **Trend Identification**: Use moving averages to identify overall sector trends. For instance, if the 50-day SMA for the Technology sector is above the 200-day SMA, it indicates a bullish trend, suggesting it's a good time to

invest.
- **Entry/Exit Points**: Crossovers can signal when to rotate into or out of sectors. For example, if the 50-day EMA crosses above the 200-day EMA for the Industrials sector, it may signal a buying opportunity.

2. Relative Strength Index (RSI)

RSI measures the speed and change of price movements, indicating overbought or oversold conditions.

- **RSI Values**: Ranges from 0 to 100. An RSI above 70 suggests overbought conditions, while an RSI below 30 suggests oversold conditions.

How to Use:

- **Overbought/Oversold Levels**: Use RSI to identify potential reversal points. A high RSI may indicate that a sector is overbought and due for a pullback, while a low RSI suggests a sector may be oversold and due for a rebound.
- **Divergence**: Look for divergence between RSI and price movements. For instance, if prices are rising but RSI is falling, it may indicate weakening momentum and a potential reversal.

Impact on Sectors:

- **Rotation Decisions**: Use RSI to identify sectors that may be overextended and due for rotation. For example, if the RSI for the Consumer Discretionary sector is above 70, it may be time to rotate out and take profits.
- **Entry Points**: A low RSI (below 30) for the Healthcare sector could signal a buying opportunity if it indicates the sector is oversold.

3. Support and Resistance Levels

Support and resistance levels indicate price points where a security tends to find buying or selling pressure.

- **Support**: A price level where buying interest is strong

enough to prevent the price from falling further.
- **Resistance**: A price level where selling interest is strong enough to prevent the price from rising further.

How to Use:
- **Trading Ranges**: Identify key support and resistance levels to determine potential entry and exit points. For instance, if the Technology sector consistently finds support around a certain price level, it may be a good entry point.
- **Breakouts**: A breakout above resistance or below support can signal a new trend. For example, if the Utilities sector breaks above a long-term resistance level, it may indicate the start of a new uptrend.

Impact on Sectors:
- **Entry/Exit Points**: Use support and resistance levels to identify potential buying or selling opportunities within sectors. For instance, if the Energy sector approaches a long-term support level, it might be a buying opportunity.
- **Trend Confirmation**: A breakout above resistance for the Financials sector could confirm a bullish trend, suggesting it's a good time to invest.

4. Volume Analysis

Volume analysis involves studying the trading volume of a security to understand the strength of price movements. High volume during price increases suggests strong buying interest, while high volume during price decreases suggests strong selling interest.

How to Use:
- **Volume Spikes**: Look for unusual spikes in volume, which can indicate strong interest and potential price movements. For example, a spike in volume in the Industrials sector could signal a significant price move.

- **Volume Trends**: Consistent increases in volume during an uptrend indicate strong buying interest, supporting the trend's sustainability. Conversely, declining volume during an uptrend may indicate weakening momentum.

Impact on Sectors:
- **Trend Strength**: Use volume analysis to confirm the strength of a sector's trend. For example, if the Technology sector is in an uptrend with increasing volume, it indicates strong buying interest and trend sustainability.
- **Reversal Signals**: A volume spike in the Consumer Staples sector during a downtrend could signal capitulation and a potential reversal.

5. Moving Average Convergence Divergence (MACD)

MACD is a trend-following momentum indicator that shows the relationship between two moving averages of a security's price. The MACD line is the difference between the 12-day EMA and the 26-day EMA, and the signal line is the 9-day EMA of the MACD line.

How to Use:
- **Crossovers**: When the MACD line crosses above the signal line, it's a bullish signal. When it crosses below, it's a bearish signal.
- **Divergence**: Look for divergence between the MACD and price. For example, if prices are making new highs but the MACD is not, it could indicate weakening momentum.

Impact on Sectors:
- **Trend Confirmation**: Use MACD crossovers to confirm sector trends. For instance, if the MACD for the Healthcare sector crosses above the signal line, it may indicate a bullish trend.
- **Entry/Exit Points**: Use MACD to time entries and exits for sector rotation. For example, a bearish MACD

crossover in the Financials sector could signal it's time to rotate out.

Fundamental Analysis for Sector Evaluation

Fundamental analysis involves evaluating a sector's financial health and growth prospects based on economic data, industry trends, and company performance.

1. Earnings Reports

Earnings reports provide insights into a company's financial performance, including revenue, profit margins, and earnings per share (EPS).

How to Use:

- **Revenue Growth**: Look for sectors with strong revenue growth, indicating robust demand. For example, strong revenue growth in the Technology sector suggests high demand for tech products and services.
- **Profit Margins**: High profit margins suggest efficient operations and pricing power. For instance, high margins in the Healthcare sector indicate strong pricing power for medical products and services.
- **EPS Trends**: Consistent EPS growth indicates financial stability and growth potential. Positive EPS trends in the Consumer Discretionary sector signal robust consumer spending and sector health.

Impact on Sectors:

- Analyze earnings reports to identify sectors with strong financial performance and growth prospects. For example, strong earnings in the Industrials sector suggest robust business investment and economic growth.

2. P/E Ratios

The price-to-earnings (P/E) ratio compares a company's stock price to its earnings per share, indicating how much investors are willing to pay for a dollar of earnings.

How to Use:

- **Comparative Analysis**: Compare P/E ratios within and across sectors to identify undervalued or overvalued sectors. For instance, if the P/E ratio for the Technology sector is significantly higher than the market average, it may indicate overvaluation.
- **Growth vs. Value**: High P/E ratios may indicate growth sectors, while low P/E ratios may suggest value opportunities. For example, a high P/E ratio in the Consumer Discretionary sector suggests investors expect strong future growth.

Impact on Sectors:

- Use P/E ratios to evaluate sector valuations and identify potential investment opportunities. For example, if the Financials sector has a low P/E ratio relative to its historical average, it may indicate an undervalued opportunity.

3. Industry Trends

Industry trends provide insights into the broader forces shaping sector performance, including technological advancements, regulatory changes, and consumer preferences.

How to Use:

- **Technological Advancements**: Identify sectors benefiting from technological innovations, such as Technology and Healthcare. For example, advancements in AI and machine learning drive growth in the Technology sector.
- **Regulatory Changes**: Assess the impact of regulatory changes on sectors like Financials and Energy. For instance, new banking regulations may affect the profitability of the Financials sector.
- **Consumer Preferences**: Monitor shifts in consumer behavior to identify growth opportunities in sectors

like Consumer Discretionary and Consumer Staples. For example, increasing demand for organic food boosts the Consumer Staples sector.

Impact on Sectors:
- Analyze industry trends to identify sectors with strong growth prospects and favorable conditions. For example, the shift towards renewable energy supports growth in the Energy sector.

4. Economic Indicators

Key economic indicators such as GDP growth, inflation rates, and interest rates provide context for evaluating sector performance.

How to Use:
- **GDP Growth**: Sectors like Technology and Industrials perform well during economic expansion. For example, strong GDP growth indicates increased business investments, benefiting the Industrials sector.
- **Inflation Rates**: Sectors like Utilities and Consumer Staples offer stability during periods of high inflation. For instance, Utilities continue to provide essential services regardless of inflationary pressures.
- **Interest Rates**: Rising rates impact sectors like Real Estate and Financials, while falling rates benefit Consumer Discretionary. For example, lower interest rates stimulate consumer spending, benefiting the Consumer Discretionary sector.

Impact on Sectors:
- Use economic indicators to assess the broader economic environment and its impact on sector performance. For example, declining interest rates may signal a favorable environment for the Real Estate sector.

Combining Technical and Fundamental Analysis

For effective sector rotation, combining technical and fundamental analysis provides a comprehensive view of market conditions and sector performance.

1. Sector Screening

Use fundamental analysis to screen for sectors with strong financial health and growth prospects.

- **Metrics**: Revenue growth, profit margins, P/E ratios, and industry trends.

2. Trend Identification

Use technical analysis to identify sector trends and potential entry/exit points.

- **Tools**: Moving averages, RSI, support and resistance levels.

3. Timing and Execution

Combine insights from both analyses to time sector rotations effectively.

- **Strategy**: Rotate into sectors with strong fundamentals and positive technical trends.

Practical Example:

1. Identify Sectors with Strong Fundamentals:

- Use earnings reports and P/E ratios to identify sectors with robust revenue growth and attractive valuations. For example, identify that the Technology sector has strong revenue growth and favorable P/E ratios.

2. Analyze Technical Trends:

- Apply moving averages and RSI to confirm positive trends and identify potential entry points. For instance, confirm that the 50-day SMA for the Technology sector is above the 200-day SMA and the RSI is in a favorable range.

3. Monitor Economic Indicators:

- Track GDP growth, inflation rates, and interest rates to assess the broader economic environment. Ensure that economic indicators support the growth outlook for the

Technology sector.

4. Execute Sector Rotation:
- Rotate into sectors with strong fundamentals and positive technical trends, adjusting the portfolio as economic conditions and market trends evolve. For example, increase exposure to the Technology sector based on favorable fundamental and technical analysis.

By using a combination of technical and fundamental analysis, investors can make informed decisions and implement effective sector rotation strategies to enhance returns and manage risks.

CHAPTER 6: CASE STUDIES

Understanding the real-world application of sector rotation strategies can provide valuable insights and practical lessons. This chapter will present detailed case studies of successful sector rotation strategies, lessons learned from past economic cycles, and analysis of real-world examples.

Successful Sector Rotation Strategies

Analyzing successful sector rotation strategies helps illustrate how investors have navigated different economic cycles and achieved superior returns.

Case Study 1: The Dot-com Boom and Bust (Late 1990s - Early 2000s)

Background:
- During the late 1990s, the Technology sector experienced unprecedented growth driven by the rise of the internet and e-commerce.
- Investors heavily favored technology stocks, leading to significant overvaluation.

Strategy:

- **Expansion Phase**: Investors rotated heavily into Technology and Telecommunications sectors as new internet-based companies emerged and flourished.
- **Peak Phase**: As valuations became stretched, savvy investors began shifting to defensive sectors like Consumer Staples and Utilities, anticipating a market correction.
- **Contraction Phase**: When the bubble burst in early 2000, Technology and Telecommunications sectors plummeted. Investors who had rotated into defensive sectors experienced less severe losses.
- **Trough Phase**: Post-crash, early adopters of cyclical recovery invested in beaten-down sectors like Financials and Industrials, positioning for the subsequent economic recovery.

Outcome:
- Investors who anticipated the peak and rotated into defensive sectors preserved capital and mitigated losses during the downturn.
- Rotating into early cyclical sectors post-crash allowed investors to capitalize on the recovery.

Lessons Learned:
- The importance of monitoring valuations and macroeconomic indicators to anticipate market peaks and troughs.
- The effectiveness of rotating into defensive sectors during economic uncertainty.

Case Study 2: The Global Financial Crisis (2007-2009)

Background:
- The financial crisis was triggered by the collapse of the housing market and widespread financial instability.
- The Financials sector was severely impacted, with significant losses in banking and real estate.

Strategy:
- **Peak Phase:** As warning signs of an overheated housing market emerged, some investors began rotating out of Financials and Real Estate into defensive sectors like Healthcare and Consumer Staples.
- **Contraction Phase:** During the crisis, defensive sectors outperformed, providing stability amidst market turmoil.
- **Trough Phase:** In the aftermath of the crisis, as economic indicators began to stabilize, investors rotated into cyclical sectors like Financials and Consumer Discretionary to capitalize on the recovery.

Outcome:
- Investors who rotated into defensive sectors ahead of the crisis experienced lower volatility and preserved capital.
- Rotating into cyclical sectors during the early recovery phase enabled investors to capture significant upside as the economy rebounded.

Lessons Learned:
- The value of early recognition of economic warning signs and proactive sector rotation.
- The importance of flexibility and readiness to rotate into cyclical sectors as recovery signals emerge.

Lessons from Past Economic Cycles

Analyzing past economic cycles provides valuable insights into sector performance and investment strategies.

The 1970s Stagflation:
- **Background:** The 1970s were marked by stagflation, a combination of high inflation and stagnant economic growth.
- **Sector Performance:** Energy and Materials sectors

outperformed due to rising commodity prices, while most other sectors struggled.
- **Strategy**: Investors who allocated to Energy and Materials sectors benefited from commodity price surges. Defensive sectors like Consumer Staples also provided stability.
- **Lessons Learned**: In periods of high inflation, sectors tied to commodities and essential goods tend to outperform.

The 1980s Economic Expansion:
- **Background**: The 1980s saw strong economic growth driven by tax cuts, deregulation, and technological advancements.
- **Sector Performance**: Technology, Financials, and Consumer Discretionary sectors thrived.
- **Strategy**: Investors who rotated into growth-oriented sectors during the expansion phase reaped substantial gains.
- **Lessons Learned**: Recognizing the drivers of economic growth and investing in sectors poised to benefit from these trends can yield significant returns.

The 2001 Recession and Recovery:
- **Background**: The early 2000s recession was triggered by the bursting of the dot-com bubble and the September 11 attacks.
- **Sector Performance**: Defensive sectors outperformed during the recession, while Technology and Telecommunications struggled.
- **Strategy**: Rotating into defensive sectors during the downturn and moving into cyclical sectors during the recovery phase proved effective.
- **Lessons Learned**: The importance of sector rotation in mitigating losses during downturns and capturing

growth during recoveries.

Analysis of Real-World Examples

Example 1: Post-2008 Financial Crisis Recovery

Background:

- Following the severe downturn of the 2008 financial crisis, the economy began a slow recovery.

Strategy:

- **Early Recovery Phase**: Investors rotated into Financials and Consumer Discretionary sectors, anticipating a rebound in consumer spending and improved financial stability.
- **Mid-Recovery Phase**: As economic indicators continued to improve, investors increased exposure to Industrials and Technology sectors.
- **Late Recovery Phase**: Defensive sectors like Healthcare and Consumer Staples were added to portfolios to mitigate potential market volatility.

Outcome:

- Early movers into cyclical sectors captured substantial gains as the economy recovered.
- Diversifying into defensive sectors later in the recovery helped manage risks and protect gains.

Example 2: The COVID-19 Pandemic (2020)

Background:

- The COVID-19 pandemic led to a sharp economic contraction and unprecedented market volatility.

Strategy:

- **Initial Shock Phase**: Investors rotated into defensive sectors like Healthcare and Consumer Staples, which remained in demand despite the economic downturn.
- **Recovery Phase**: As vaccines were developed and economic recovery began, investors rotated into cyclical

sectors like Consumer Discretionary, Industrials, and Technology, which benefited from pent-up demand and increased spending.

Outcome:
- Defensive sectors provided stability during the initial market shock.
- Cyclical sectors offered significant upside as the economy began to recover.

Lessons Learned:
- The importance of being nimble and adapting sector allocations in response to rapid economic changes.
- The value of diversifying across sectors to manage risks during periods of extreme uncertainty.

By examining these real-world examples and case studies, investors can gain a deeper understanding of how sector rotation strategies can be effectively implemented in various economic conditions. These insights can help in making informed decisions and optimizing portfolio performance.

CHAPTER 7: ADVANCED TECHNIQUES

For those who seek to elevate their investment game and maximize the potential of their portfolios, delving deeper into advanced sector rotation strategies is essential. While basic sector rotation can significantly enhance returns and manage risks, advanced techniques open up new avenues for optimization and precision. This chapter will take you beyond the fundamentals, exploring how to combine sector rotation with other powerful investment strategies, effectively utilize Exchange-Traded Funds (ETFs) and mutual funds, and implement sophisticated risk management and diversification methods.

Imagine having the ability to not only anticipate market movements but also strategically position your investments to capitalize on these shifts with surgical precision. This is the promise of advanced sector rotation strategies. By integrating momentum, value, and growth investing principles, you can create a multi-faceted approach that leverages the strengths of each method. Using ETFs and mutual funds, you can gain diversified exposure to specific sectors with ease and efficiency, all while benefiting from professional management and low costs.

Moreover, advanced risk management techniques such as dynamic asset allocation, hedging, and the strategic use of stop-loss orders provide a robust defense against market volatility and unforeseen downturns. These tools enable you to protect your capital and lock in gains, ensuring that your portfolio remains resilient in the face of market turbulence.

Whether you are an experienced investor looking to refine your strategies or a curious novice eager to learn the intricacies of high-level investing, this chapter will equip you with the knowledge and tools to take your sector rotation strategies to the next level. Dive in, and discover how advanced techniques can transform your approach to investing, offering greater control, enhanced returns, and a more secure financial future.

Combining Sector Rotation with Other Strategies

Integrating sector rotation with other investment strategies can enhance portfolio performance and provide additional layers of risk management.

1. Momentum Investing

Momentum investing involves buying securities that have shown an upward price trend and selling those with downward trends. This strategy can be effectively combined with sector rotation.

- **Strategy**: Identify sectors that have demonstrated strong recent performance and rotate into these sectors. Conversely, rotate out of sectors showing weak performance.
- **Tools**: Use technical indicators like moving averages, RSI, and MACD to identify momentum trends within sectors.
- **Example**: During an expansion phase, rotate into sectors like Technology and Consumer Discretionary that are showing strong momentum.

Benefits:
- Capitalizes on short-term trends to enhance returns.
- Reduces exposure to underperforming sectors.

Challenges:
- Requires active monitoring and frequent adjustments.
- May incur higher transaction costs.

2. Value Investing

Value investing involves selecting stocks that appear to be undervalued based on fundamental analysis. Combining this with sector rotation can identify undervalued sectors poised for recovery.

- **Strategy**: Use valuation metrics such as P/E ratios, price-to-book ratios, and dividend yields to identify undervalued sectors.
- **Tools**: Fundamental analysis tools to assess sector valuations.
- **Example**: During a contraction phase, rotate into sectors like Financials or Industrials that are undervalued but have strong recovery potential.

Benefits:
- Potential to buy sectors at a discount and benefit from their eventual recovery.
- Provides a margin of safety by focusing on fundamentally sound sectors.

Challenges:
- Requires thorough fundamental analysis.
- Value sectors may remain undervalued for extended periods.

3. Growth Investing

Growth investing focuses on companies or sectors expected to grow at an above-average rate compared to others. This can complement sector rotation by identifying high-growth sectors

during expansion phases.
- **Strategy**: Rotate into sectors with strong growth prospects, such as Technology or Healthcare, during economic expansions.
- **Tools**: Analyze earnings growth rates, revenue growth, and industry trends.
- **Example**: In a recovering economy, focus on growth sectors that are likely to benefit from increased consumer spending and technological advancements.

Benefits:
- Captures significant upside potential in high-growth sectors.
- Aligns with economic phases where growth is favored.

Challenges:
- Growth sectors can be volatile and carry higher risk.
- Requires ongoing analysis to identify and verify growth prospects.

Utilizing ETFs and Mutual Funds for Sector Rotation

Exchange-Traded Funds (ETFs) and mutual funds provide an efficient way to implement sector rotation strategies, offering diversification and ease of trading.

1. Sector ETFs

Sector ETFs are designed to track specific sectors, providing targeted exposure without the need to pick individual stocks.

- **Benefits**:
  - **Diversification**: ETFs typically hold a basket of stocks within a sector, reducing idiosyncratic risk.
  - **Liquidity**: ETFs trade like stocks, allowing for quick and easy adjustments to sector allocations.
  - **Cost-Effective**: Lower expense ratios compared

to actively managed mutual funds.
- **Examples:**
  - **Technology Select Sector SPDR Fund (XLK):** Provides exposure to the Technology sector.
  - **Consumer Discretionary Select Sector SPDR Fund (XLY):** Tracks the Consumer Discretionary sector.
  - **Health Care Select Sector SPDR Fund (XLV):** Focuses on the Healthcare sector.

2. Sector Mutual Funds

Sector mutual funds are actively managed funds that invest in specific sectors. They offer professional management but typically come with higher fees.

- **Benefits:**
  - **Professional Management:** Fund managers actively select stocks within the sector, potentially outperforming passive ETFs.
  - **Research and Insights:** Access to in-depth research and insights from professional managers.
- **Examples:**
  - **Fidelity Select Technology Portfolio (FSPTX):** Actively managed fund focusing on the Technology sector.
  - **Vanguard Health Care Fund (VGHCX):** Managed fund providing exposure to the Healthcare sector.
  - **T. Rowe Price Financial Services Fund (PRISX):** Focuses on the Financials sector.

Choosing Between ETFs and Mutual Funds

- **Consider ETFs:** If you prefer lower costs, ease of trading, and broad diversification.

- **Consider Mutual Funds**: If you value professional management and are willing to pay higher fees for potential outperformance.

Risk Management and Diversification

Effective risk management and diversification are critical components of successful sector rotation strategies.

1. Portfolio Diversification

Diversifying across sectors helps mitigate risks associated with any single sector's underperformance.

- **Strategy**: Maintain exposure to multiple sectors to reduce idiosyncratic risk. Adjust allocations based on economic phases but avoid over-concentration in any one sector.
- **Example**: During an expansion phase, you might allocate 40% to growth sectors like Technology and Consumer Discretionary, 30% to cyclical sectors like Industrials and Financials, and 30% to defensive sectors like Healthcare and Utilities.

Benefits:
- Reduces portfolio volatility.
- Protects against sector-specific downturns.

Challenges:
- May limit potential upside if certain sectors significantly outperform.
- Requires ongoing monitoring and rebalancing.

2. Hedging Strategies

Hedging involves using financial instruments to offset potential losses in the portfolio.

- **Strategy**: Use options, futures, or inverse ETFs to hedge against sector-specific risks.
- **Examples**:
    - **Put Options**: Buy put options on sector ETFs to

protect against downside risk.
- **Inverse ETFs**: Invest in inverse ETFs that move opposite to the sector's performance, providing a hedge against sector declines.

Benefits:
- Provides downside protection.
- Reduces overall portfolio risk.

Challenges:
- Hedging can be complex and requires understanding of financial instruments.
- May incur additional costs and reduce potential returns.

3. Dynamic Asset Allocation

Dynamic asset allocation involves adjusting sector allocations based on changing economic conditions and market dynamics.

- **Strategy**: Regularly review and adjust sector allocations to reflect current economic indicators and market trends.
- **Example**: Increase allocation to defensive sectors during economic uncertainty and shift to cyclical sectors during recovery phases.

Benefits:
- Enhances flexibility to respond to market changes.
- Optimizes portfolio performance across different economic phases.

Challenges:
- Requires active management and constant monitoring.
- May lead to higher transaction costs.

4. Stop-Loss Orders

Using stop-loss orders can help protect gains and limit losses.

- **Strategy**: Set stop-loss orders on sector ETFs or stocks to automatically sell if the price falls below a certain level.

- **Example**: If you hold a Technology sector ETF and set a stop-loss order 10% below the purchase price, the ETF will be sold if its price drops by 10%.

Benefits:
- Limits potential losses.
- Provides automatic risk management without constant monitoring.

Challenges:
- Stop-loss orders may be triggered by short-term market volatility.
- Could result in selling during temporary downturns, missing potential recoveries.

Practical Considerations

1. Costs and Tax Implications
- **Transaction Costs**: Frequent trading can incur higher transaction costs. Consider using low-cost ETFs to minimize expenses.
- **Tax Implications**: Short-term capital gains are taxed at higher rates than long-term gains. Be mindful of the tax implications of frequent sector rotation.

2. Rebalancing
- **Regular Rebalancing**: Periodically review and rebalance the portfolio to maintain desired sector allocations and manage risks.
- **Example**: Quarterly rebalancing can help ensure that the portfolio stays aligned with your investment strategy and economic outlook.

3. Monitoring and Adjustments
- **Continuous Monitoring**: Regularly review economic indicators, market trends, and sector performance to make informed adjustments.
- **Example**: Set up alerts for key economic data releases

and sector performance updates to stay informed and make timely decisions.

4. Risk Tolerance and Time Horizon

- **Risk Tolerance**: Consider your risk tolerance when implementing advanced strategies. Higher risk strategies like momentum investing may not be suitable for all investors.

- **Time Horizon**: Align sector rotation strategies with your investment time horizon. Long-term investors may prefer strategic rotation, while short-term traders might focus on tactical rotation.

By integrating advanced techniques, utilizing ETFs and mutual funds, and implementing robust risk management and diversification strategies, investors can enhance their sector rotation strategies and optimize portfolio performance.

CHAPTER 8: PRACTICAL CONSIDERATIONS

While understanding the theory and strategies behind sector rotation is crucial, implementing these strategies successfully requires careful attention to practical details. This chapter will guide you through the essential practical considerations for building and managing a sector rotation portfolio, understanding costs and tax implications, and avoiding common pitfalls.

◆ ◆ ◆

Building and Managing a Sector Rotation Portfolio

Constructing and maintaining a sector rotation portfolio involves several key steps. Here's a detailed guide to help you build and manage your portfolio effectively.

1. Define Your Investment Goals and Risk Tolerance

Before building your portfolio, it's essential to establish clear investment goals and assess your risk tolerance.

- **Investment Goals**: Determine your primary objectives, such as capital appreciation, income generation, or a combination of both. Consider your investment horizon and financial goals.

- **Risk Tolerance**: Assess how much risk you're willing to take on. This will influence your sector allocation and the aggressiveness of your rotation strategy.

Example: If your goal is long-term capital appreciation with moderate risk, you might allocate a larger portion to growth sectors during expansions and rotate into defensive sectors during downturns.

2. Select the Right Sectors

Choose sectors that align with your economic outlook and investment strategy. Diversify across sectors to manage risk and optimize returns.

- **Economic Phases**: Allocate to sectors that perform well during specific economic phases. For example, Technology and Consumer Discretionary during expansions, and Healthcare and Utilities during contractions.
- **Diversification**: Ensure your portfolio is diversified to mitigate sector-specific risks. Avoid over-concentration in any single sector.

Example: During an economic expansion, you might allocate 30% to Technology, 25% to Consumer Discretionary, 20% to Industrials, 15% to Financials, and 10% to Healthcare.

3. Choose Your Investment Vehicles

Decide whether to use individual stocks, ETFs, or mutual funds to implement your sector rotation strategy.

- **Individual Stocks**: Allows for precise selection but requires extensive research and monitoring.
- **ETFs**: Provide diversified exposure to sectors with lower costs and ease of trading. Ideal for broad sector bets.
- **Mutual Funds**: Offer professional management but typically come with higher fees.

Example: If you prefer a hands-off approach, use sector ETFs to gain broad exposure to desired sectors. For a more hands-on strategy, select individual stocks within those sectors.

4. Monitor Economic Indicators and Sector Performance

Regularly review key economic indicators and sector performance to inform your rotation decisions.

- **Indicators**: Track GDP growth, employment data, inflation rates, consumer confidence, and interest rates.
- **Sector Analysis**: Use technical and fundamental analysis to evaluate sector trends and performance.

Example: If GDP growth is strong and consumer confidence is high, you might increase exposure to Consumer Discretionary and Industrials. Conversely, if inflation rates are rising and economic growth is slowing, shift towards Healthcare and Consumer Staples.

5. Implement and Adjust Your Strategy

Execute your sector rotation strategy based on your analysis and regularly adjust your portfolio to reflect changing economic conditions.

- **Entry and Exit Points**: Use technical analysis tools like moving averages, RSI, and support/resistance levels to time your entries and exits.
- **Rebalancing**: Periodically review and rebalance your portfolio to maintain desired sector allocations.

Example: Set a quarterly review schedule to assess your portfolio's performance and rebalance as needed. Adjust sector allocations based on updated economic data and market trends.

Costs and Tax Implications

Understanding the costs and tax implications of sector rotation is crucial for maximizing returns and minimizing liabilities.

1. Transaction Costs

Frequent trading can incur higher transaction costs, impacting overall returns.

- **Commissions**: Fees charged by brokers for buying and selling securities. Opt for brokers with low commission rates to reduce costs.
- **Bid-Ask Spread**: The difference between the buying and selling price of a security. Higher spreads can increase trading costs, especially for less liquid assets.

Example: If you frequently trade sector ETFs, choose a brokerage with low commission fees and narrow bid-ask spreads to minimize transaction costs.

2. Expense Ratios

Expense ratios are the annual fees charged by ETFs and mutual funds, expressed as a percentage of assets under management.

- **Low-Cost ETFs**: Select ETFs with low expense ratios to reduce annual costs and enhance net returns.
- **Actively Managed Funds**: Be aware that actively managed mutual funds typically have higher expense ratios. Ensure the potential for outperformance justifies the higher costs.

Example: Compare the expense ratios of sector ETFs and choose those with the lowest fees while providing adequate sector exposure.

3. Tax Implications

Frequent trading can have tax implications, particularly with short-term capital gains.

- **Short-Term vs. Long-Term Gains**: Short-term capital gains (assets held for less than a year) are taxed at higher rates than long-term gains (assets held for more than a year). Plan your trades to benefit from favorable tax treatment.
- **Tax-Efficient Investing**: Use tax-advantaged accounts like IRAs or 401(k)s to defer taxes on gains. Consider tax-loss harvesting to offset gains with losses.

Example: Hold investments for over a year whenever possible to benefit from lower long-term capital gains tax rates. Utilize tax-advantaged accounts to shelter gains from immediate taxation.

Common Pitfalls and How to Avoid Them

Successfully implementing sector rotation strategies involves avoiding common mistakes that can undermine your efforts.

1. Overtrading

Frequent trading can lead to higher transaction costs, increased taxes, and reduced returns.

- **Solution**: Develop a disciplined strategy and stick to it. Avoid making impulsive trades based on short-term market movements.

Example: Set predefined criteria for entering and exiting sector positions, and resist the temptation to deviate based on market noise.

2. Ignoring Diversification

Over-concentration in a single sector can expose your portfolio to significant risk.

- **Solution**: Ensure your portfolio is diversified across multiple sectors to mitigate sector-specific risks.

Example: Even if you are bullish on Technology, maintain exposure to defensive sectors like Healthcare and Consumer Staples to balance your portfolio.

3. Failing to Monitor and Adjust

Neglecting to regularly review and adjust your portfolio can result in misaligned sector allocations and missed opportunities.

- **Solution**: Schedule regular portfolio reviews to assess performance and make necessary adjustments based on updated economic data and market conditions.

Example: Conduct quarterly reviews to rebalance your portfolio, ensuring it remains aligned with your sector rotation strategy and economic outlook.

4. Over-Reliance on Economic Indicators

Relying solely on economic indicators without considering other factors can lead to suboptimal decisions.

- **Solution**: Use a combination of economic indicators, technical analysis, and fundamental analysis to inform your sector rotation decisions.

Example: In addition to monitoring GDP growth and inflation rates, analyze sector-specific fundamentals and technical trends to make well-rounded investment decisions.

5. Emotional Investing

Letting emotions drive your investment decisions can lead to poor outcomes.

- **Solution**: Develop a disciplined, rule-based strategy and stick to it, regardless of market conditions. Keep emotions in check by focusing on long-term goals.

Example: Establish a set of rules for sector rotation and adhere to them, even during periods of market volatility or uncertainty.

By addressing these practical considerations, investors can build and manage a sector rotation portfolio more effectively, optimize returns, and avoid common pitfalls.

CHAPTER 9: FUTURE TRENDS IN SECTOR ROTATION

As the global economy continues to evolve, so too do the strategies and tools available for sector rotation. This chapter explores emerging trends that may shape the future of sector rotation, including the impact of technological advancements, the increasing importance of sustainability and ESG (Environmental, Social, and Governance) criteria, and the role of global economic integration.

Technological Advancements

Technology is revolutionizing the investment landscape, providing new tools and methods for implementing sector rotation strategies.

1. Artificial Intelligence and Machine Learning

AI and machine learning are transforming how investors analyze data and make decisions.

- **Data Analysis**: AI algorithms can process vast amounts of data, identifying patterns and trends that might be missed by human analysts. These insights can enhance sector rotation strategies by providing more accurate and timely information.

- **Predictive Modeling**: Machine learning models can predict economic cycles and sector performance with greater accuracy, allowing for more precise timing of sector rotations.

Example: An AI-driven platform might analyze global economic indicators, news sentiment, and historical performance data to predict the next economic phase and suggest optimal sector allocations.

2. Big Data

The availability of big data is enabling more informed investment decisions.

- **Alternative Data Sources**: Investors are increasingly using alternative data sources such as social media activity, satellite imagery, and transaction data to gain insights into sector performance.
- **Real-Time Data**: Access to real-time data allows investors to make quicker and more informed decisions, adjusting their sector allocations as new information becomes available.

Example: Analyzing social media trends to gauge consumer sentiment towards different sectors or using satellite imagery to assess industrial activity levels.

3. Automated Trading and Robo-Advisors

Automation is making sector rotation more accessible and efficient.

- **Robo-Advisors**: These platforms use algorithms to create and manage portfolios based on predefined strategies, including sector rotation. They offer a low-cost, hands-off approach to implementing sector rotation.

- **Automated Trading Systems**: These systems can execute trades based on specific criteria, ensuring timely and efficient sector rotations without the need for constant manual intervention.

Example: A robo-advisor might automatically adjust your sector allocations based on changes in economic indicators or market conditions.

Sustainability and ESG Criteria

The growing importance of sustainability and ESG factors is reshaping investment strategies, including sector rotation.

1. ESG Integration

Investors are increasingly incorporating ESG criteria into their investment decisions.

- **ESG Ratings**: Companies and sectors are evaluated based on their environmental, social, and governance practices. These ratings influence investment decisions, as investors seek to align their portfolios with their values.
- **Sustainable Sectors**: Sectors that score highly on ESG criteria, such as renewable energy and healthcare, are attracting more investment.

Example: Integrating ESG ratings into your sector rotation strategy might lead to increased allocations to sectors like renewable energy, which are expected to benefit from the transition to a low-carbon economy.

2. Impact Investing

Impact investing focuses on generating positive social and environmental outcomes alongside financial returns.

- **Thematic Investments**: Investors are increasingly looking for opportunities in sectors that address global challenges, such as climate change, healthcare, and clean technology.
- **Long-Term Growth**: Sectors that contribute to

sustainability and social well-being are expected to experience long-term growth, making them attractive for sector rotation strategies.

Example: Rotating into sectors like clean energy and sustainable agriculture, which are expected to benefit from increased demand for sustainable solutions.

Global Economic Integration

As the global economy becomes more interconnected, investors must consider international factors when implementing sector rotation strategies.

1. Cross-Border Investments

Global economic integration means that sector performance can be influenced by international trends and events.

- **Global Diversification**: Diversifying across international sectors can reduce risk and enhance returns by taking advantage of growth opportunities in different regions.
- **Currency Risk**: When investing internationally, consider the impact of currency fluctuations on sector performance.

Example: Investing in emerging market sectors that are poised for growth due to favorable economic conditions and demographic trends.

2. Trade Policies and Geopolitical Risks

Trade policies and geopolitical events can significantly impact sector performance.

- **Trade Agreements**: Changes in trade agreements can affect sectors differently, creating opportunities for sector rotation.
- **Geopolitical Tensions**: Geopolitical risks, such as conflicts or political instability, can disrupt global supply chains and affect sector performance.

Example: Rotating out of sectors heavily impacted by trade tensions and into sectors less affected by geopolitical risks.

3. Technological Transfer and Innovation

The transfer of technology and innovation across borders influences global sector dynamics.

- **Tech-Driven Growth**: Sectors benefiting from technological advancements in multiple regions can offer attractive investment opportunities.
- **Collaboration and Competition**: International collaboration and competition in technology can drive sector growth and create new investment opportunities.

Example: Investing in sectors like biotechnology or artificial intelligence that are experiencing rapid innovation globally.

Adapting to Future Trends

To stay ahead of the curve, investors must adapt their sector rotation strategies to incorporate these emerging trends.

1. Embrace Technological Tools

Utilize AI, big data, and automated trading systems to enhance your sector rotation strategies.

- **AI and Machine Learning**: Integrate AI-driven platforms to analyze data and predict economic cycles more accurately.
- **Big Data**: Leverage alternative data sources for deeper insights into sector performance.

Example: Use a machine learning platform to continuously analyze economic indicators and market trends, providing real-time recommendations for sector rotations.

2. Integrate ESG Criteria

Incorporate sustainability and ESG factors into your investment decisions to align with global trends and investor preferences.

- **ESG Ratings**: Use ESG ratings to identify sectors with strong sustainability practices.
- **Impact Investing**: Allocate to sectors that contribute to

positive social and environmental outcomes.

Example: Develop a sector rotation strategy that prioritizes sectors with high ESG ratings and strong long-term growth potential.

3. Consider Global Perspectives

Factor in global economic integration, trade policies, and geopolitical risks when making sector rotation decisions.

- **Global Diversification**: Diversify your portfolio across international sectors to mitigate risk and capture global growth opportunities.
- **Geopolitical Analysis**: Stay informed about geopolitical developments and their potential impact on sector performance.

Example: Regularly review global economic reports and geopolitical analysis to inform your sector rotation strategy and make adjustments as needed.

By staying informed and adapting to these emerging trends, investors can enhance their sector rotation strategies and position their portfolios for future success. Embracing technological advancements, integrating ESG criteria, and considering global economic factors will be key to navigating the evolving investment landscape.

CHAPTER 10: CREATING A SECTOR ROTATION PLAN

Creating a sector rotation plan involves a detailed process of setting goals, understanding the economic cycle, selecting sectors, and continuously monitoring and adjusting your strategy. This chapter will guide you through the steps to create a comprehensive and effective sector rotation plan tailored to your investment objectives.

Step 1: Setting Investment Goals and Risk Tolerance

The foundation of any investment plan is understanding your goals and risk tolerance. This will influence your sector choices and the aggressiveness of your rotation strategy.

1. Define Your Investment Goals

- **Capital Appreciation**: Focus on sectors with high growth potential.
- **Income Generation**: Prioritize sectors known for high dividend yields.
- **Balanced Approach**: Combine both growth and income-

focused sectors.

Example: If your goal is long-term capital appreciation, you might focus on sectors like Technology and Healthcare, which have strong growth prospects.

2. Assess Your Risk Tolerance

- **Aggressive**: Higher risk for potentially higher returns, willing to endure volatility.
- **Moderate**: Balanced approach, willing to take on some risk but prefers a mix of stable and growth sectors.
- **Conservative**: Lower risk tolerance, prioritizing capital preservation and income over high returns.

Example: If you have a moderate risk tolerance, you might balance your portfolio with a mix of growth sectors (like Consumer Discretionary) and defensive sectors (like Consumer Staples).

Step 2: Understanding the Economic Cycle

To effectively rotate sectors, you need to understand the different phases of the economic cycle and how they impact sector performance.

1. Identify Economic Phases

- **Expansion**: Increasing GDP, rising employment, higher consumer spending.
- **Peak**: Maximum economic output, rising inflation, potential for economic slowdown.
- **Contraction**: Decreasing GDP, rising unemployment, reduced consumer spending.
- **Trough**: Lowest point of economic activity, early signs of recovery.

Example: During an expansion phase, sectors like Technology and Industrials typically outperform due to increased consumer and business spending.

2. Monitor Key Economic Indicators

- **GDP Growth**
- **Employment Data**
- **Inflation Rates**
- **Consumer Confidence**
- **Interest Rates**

Example: A rise in consumer confidence and GDP growth signals an expansion phase, prompting a shift towards growth-oriented sectors.

Step 3: Selecting Sectors for Each Phase

Based on your understanding of the economic cycle, choose sectors that historically perform well during each phase.

1. Expansion Phase

- **Technology**
- **Consumer Discretionary**
- **Industrials**

Example: Allocate a significant portion of your portfolio to Technology and Consumer Discretionary sectors during an expansion phase to capitalize on increased spending.

2. Peak Phase

- **Healthcare**
- **Utilities**
- **Consumer Staples**

Example: As the economy reaches its peak, shift to defensive sectors like Healthcare and Consumer Staples to protect against potential downturns.

3. Contraction Phase

- **Consumer Staples**
- **Utilities**
- **Healthcare**

Example: During a contraction, maintain a higher allocation to Consumer Staples and Utilities, which provide essential goods and services with stable demand.

4. Trough Phase

- **Financials**
- **Consumer Discretionary**
- **Industrials**

Example: In the early stages of recovery, rotate into Financials and Industrials to benefit from improving economic conditions and increased lending activity.

Step 4: Implementing Your Strategy

With your sector allocations defined for each economic phase, it's time to implement your strategy.

1. Choose Investment Vehicles

- **ETFs**: For broad sector exposure with lower costs.
- **Mutual Funds**: For professional management and targeted sector strategies.
- **Individual Stocks**: For precise selection and potentially higher returns.

Example: Use sector-specific ETFs like the Technology Select Sector SPDR Fund (XLK) for broad exposure to the Technology sector during an expansion phase.

2. Set Entry and Exit Points

- **Technical Analysis**: Use tools like moving averages, RSI, and MACD to identify optimal entry and exit points.
- **Fundamental Analysis**: Assess sector fundamentals to ensure sound investments.

Example: Enter a sector when its 50-day moving average crosses above the 200-day moving average, indicating an upward trend.

3. Diversify Your Portfolio

- **Sector Diversification**: Allocate across multiple sectors to mitigate risk.
- **Geographic Diversification**: Consider international sectors to further reduce risk and capture global growth

opportunities.

Example: Along with U.S. sectors, allocate a portion to emerging market sectors poised for growth.

Step 5: Monitoring and Adjusting Your Plan

Continuous monitoring and adjustments are crucial for maintaining an effective sector rotation strategy.

1. Regular Portfolio Reviews

- **Frequency**: Schedule quarterly or bi-annual reviews to assess performance and rebalance your portfolio.
- **Performance Metrics**: Track sector performance against benchmarks and your investment goals.

Example: During quarterly reviews, compare your portfolio's performance to relevant sector indices and adjust allocations as needed.

2. Stay Informed

- **Economic News**: Keep abreast of economic reports, central bank announcements, and geopolitical events.
- **Sector Trends**: Monitor industry developments, technological advancements, and regulatory changes.

Example: Subscribe to financial news services and economic reports to stay updated on market conditions and sector trends.

3. Make Timely Adjustments

- **Rebalancing**: Adjust sector allocations based on changing economic conditions and performance.
- **Risk Management**: Use stop-loss orders and hedging strategies to protect against downside risk.

Example: If economic indicators suggest an approaching contraction, increase allocations to defensive sectors like Utilities and Consumer Staples.

4. Learn and Adapt

- **Post-Analysis**: Analyze your past decisions to understand what worked and what didn't. Use these

insights to refine your strategy.
- **Continuous Improvement**: Stay open to new strategies, tools, and techniques to enhance your sector rotation plan.

Example: After each economic cycle, review your performance and identify areas for improvement, such as better timing of sector rotations or more effective use of technical analysis tools.

Step 6: Risk Management and Tax Considerations

Managing risk and understanding tax implications are essential for maintaining a healthy sector rotation portfolio.

1. Risk Management
- **Diversification**: Spread your investments across various sectors and asset classes to reduce risk.
- **Hedging**: Use financial instruments like options or inverse ETFs to hedge against sector-specific risks.
- **Stop-Loss Orders**: Set stop-loss orders to limit potential losses and protect gains.

Example: Implement stop-loss orders on sector ETFs to automatically sell if the price drops by a predetermined percentage.

2. Tax Considerations
- **Short-Term vs. Long-Term Gains**: Be mindful of holding periods to benefit from lower long-term capital gains tax rates.
- **Tax-Efficient Investing**: Utilize tax-advantaged accounts like IRAs or 401(k)s to defer taxes on gains. Consider tax-loss harvesting to offset gains with losses.
- **Tax Implications of Trading**: Understand the tax impact of frequent trading and plan your sector rotations accordingly.

Example: Hold investments for more than a year whenever possible to qualify for long-term capital gains tax rates and use tax-advantaged accounts to shelter gains from immediate taxation.

By following these steps, you can create a comprehensive sector rotation plan that aligns with your investment goals and risk tolerance. Regular monitoring and adjustments, combined with effective risk management and tax planning, will help you optimize your portfolio's performance across different economic phases.

CONCLUSION

Sector rotation is a sophisticated investment strategy that can significantly enhance portfolio performance by leveraging the economic cycles. By understanding and implementing sector rotation strategies, investors can optimize returns, manage risks, and navigate market volatility more effectively. This concluding chapter summarizes the key points discussed throughout the book and provides final thoughts on mastering sector rotation strategies.

Key Takeaways

1. Understanding Economic Cycles

- **Phases of the Economic Cycle**: Recognize the four main phases—expansion, peak, contraction, and trough—and their characteristics.
- **Indicators**: Monitor key economic indicators such as GDP growth, employment data, inflation rates, consumer confidence, and interest rates to identify the current phase.

2. Sector Performance in Different Phases

- **Expansion Phase**: Technology, Consumer Discretionary, and Industrials sectors typically outperform.
- **Peak Phase**: Defensive sectors like Healthcare, Utilities,

and Consumer Staples provide stability.
- **Contraction Phase**: Consumer Staples, Utilities, and Healthcare sectors are more resilient.
- **Trough Phase**: Financials, Consumer Discretionary, and Industrials sectors lead the recovery.

3. Analytical Tools and Indicators

- **Technical Analysis**: Utilize tools such as moving averages, RSI, MACD, support and resistance levels, and volume analysis to identify trends and entry/exit points.
- **Fundamental Analysis**: Evaluate sector fundamentals using earnings reports, P/E ratios, industry trends, and economic indicators.

4. Advanced Techniques

- **Combining Strategies**: Integrate momentum, value, and growth investing principles to enhance sector rotation strategies.
- **Utilizing ETFs and Mutual Funds**: Use sector-specific ETFs and mutual funds for diversified exposure and professional management.
- **Risk Management**: Implement diversification, hedging, dynamic asset allocation, and stop-loss orders to manage risks effectively.

5. Practical Considerations

- **Building and Managing a Portfolio**: Define investment goals and risk tolerance, select appropriate sectors, choose investment vehicles, and set entry and exit points.
- **Costs and Tax Implications**: Be aware of transaction costs, expense ratios, and tax implications of frequent trading.
- **Monitoring and Adjusting**: Regularly review and rebalance the portfolio based on economic conditions and performance.

6. Future Trends

- **Technological Advancements**: Leverage AI, big data, and automated trading systems to enhance sector rotation strategies.
- **Sustainability and ESG**: Incorporate ESG criteria into investment decisions to align with global trends and investor preferences.
- **Global Economic Integration**: Consider international factors, trade policies, and geopolitical risks in sector rotation decisions.

Final Thoughts

Sector rotation is not a static strategy but a dynamic approach that requires continuous learning, adaptation, and vigilance. The investment landscape is ever-evolving, and staying informed about economic developments, market trends, and technological advancements is crucial for success.

By mastering sector rotation strategies, investors can achieve a more resilient and diversified portfolio, capable of weathering various economic conditions. Whether you are a seasoned investor or a novice, the principles and techniques outlined in this book provide a solid foundation for implementing effective sector rotation strategies.

Action Steps for Investors

1. Develop a Plan

- **Define Goals**: Clearly outline your investment objectives and risk tolerance.
- **Create a Strategy**: Develop a sector rotation strategy based on economic phases and indicators.
- **Select Tools**: Choose the appropriate analytical tools and investment vehicles.

2. Stay Informed

- **Monitor Indicators**: Regularly review economic data and market trends.

- **Adapt to Changes**: Be prepared to adjust your strategy based on new information and evolving market conditions.

3. Implement and Review

- **Execute Strategy**: Implement your sector rotation plan and make trades based on your analysis.
- **Review Performance**: Continuously monitor your portfolio's performance and make adjustments as needed.
- **Learn and Improve**: Analyze your successes and failures to refine your strategy over time.

By following these action steps and maintaining a disciplined approach, you can harness the power of sector rotation to achieve your investment goals and build a robust, future-ready portfolio.

Thank you for exploring the intricacies of sector rotation with us. May your investment journey be fruitful and your strategies ever-evolving.

REFERENCES

- Burton G. Malkiel, "A Random Walk Down Wall Street", W.W. Norton & Company, 2019.
- Michael J. Mauboussin, "More Than You Know: Finding Financial Wisdom in Unconventional Places", Columbia University Press, 2006.
- Charles D. Kirkpatrick II, Julie R. Dahlquist, "Technical Analysis: The Complete Resource for Financial Market Technicians", FT Press, 2010.
- CFA Institute, "Investment Analysis and Portfolio Management", CFA Program Curriculum, CFA Institute.
- MSCI and S&P Dow Jones Indices, "Global Industry Classification Standard (GICS) Methodology".
- FTSE Russell, "Industry Classification Benchmark (ICB) Methodology".
- U.S. Census Bureau, "North American Industry Classification System (NAICS)".
- U.S. Securities and Exchange Commission (SEC), "Standard Industrial Classification (SIC)".
- Benjamin Graham, "The Intelligent Investor", Harper Business, 2006.

GLOSSARY

A

Asset Allocation: The process of dividing investments among different asset categories, such as stocks, bonds, and cash, to optimize risk and return.

B

Bear Market: A market condition in which the prices of securities are falling, leading to widespread pessimism and negative sentiment.

Bull Market: A market condition in which the prices of securities are rising, leading to widespread optimism and positive sentiment.

C

Coincident Indicators: Economic indicators that reflect the current state of the economy, such as GDP, employment levels, and income levels.

Contraction: The phase of the economic cycle characterized by decreasing economic activity, rising unemployment, and reduced consumer and business spending.

D

Defensive Sectors: Sectors that provide essential goods and services, such as Healthcare, Utilities, and Consumer Staples, which tend to perform well during economic downturns.

Diversification: The practice of spreading investments across different sectors, asset classes, or geographic regions to reduce risk.

E

Economic Cycle: The natural fluctuation of the economy between periods of expansion and contraction.

Earnings Per Share (EPS): A company's profit divided by its number of outstanding shares, indicating the profitability of the company.

Exchange-Traded Fund (ETF): A type of investment fund that is traded on stock exchanges, holding assets such as stocks, commodities, or bonds, and typically tracking an index.

F

Fundamental Analysis: The method of evaluating a security by examining financial data, such as earnings, revenue, and profit margins, as well as economic indicators and industry conditions.

G

Gross Domestic Product (GDP): The total value of goods and services produced within a country over a specific period, indicating the overall economic health.

H

Hedging: The use of financial instruments, such as options or futures, to offset potential losses in an investment portfolio.

I

Inflation: The rate at which the general price level of goods and services rises, eroding purchasing power.

L

Lagging Indicators: Economic indicators that reflect past economic performance, such as unemployment rates, corporate profits, and interest rates.

Leading Indicators: Economic indicators that predict future economic activity, such as stock market performance, manufacturing activity, and new business startups.

M

Moving Average (MA): A statistical calculation used to analyze data points by creating a series of averages of different subsets of the full data set, commonly used to identify trends.

Momentum Investing: An investment strategy that involves buying securities that have shown an upward price trend and selling those with downward trends.

P

Peak: The phase of the economic cycle characterized by the highest point of economic activity before a downturn, with rising inflation and potential economic slowdown.

Price-to-Earnings (P/E) Ratio: A valuation ratio of a company's current share price compared to its earnings per share, indicating how much investors are willing to pay for a dollar of earnings.

R

Relative Strength Index (RSI): A momentum oscillator that measures the speed and change of price movements, indicating overbought or oversold conditions.

S

Sector Rotation: An investment strategy that involves shifting investments across different sectors of the economy to capitalize on economic cycles.

Stop-Loss Order: An order to sell a security when it reaches a certain price, used to limit potential losses.

Support and Resistance Levels: Price points where a security tends to find buying or selling pressure, indicating potential entry and exit points.

T

Technical Analysis: The method of evaluating securities by analyzing statistical trends from trading activity, such as price movements and volume.

Trough: The phase of the economic cycle characterized by the lowest point of economic activity, followed by recovery signals.

U

Utilities: A defensive sector that provides essential services like electricity, water, and natural gas, known for stable demand and predictable revenue streams.

V

Volume Analysis: The study of trading volume to understand the strength of price movements and identify potential reversals.

Y

Yield Curve: A graph that plots the interest rates of bonds with equal credit quality but different maturity dates, used to predict economic changes.

www.ingramcontent.com/pod-product-compliance
Lightning Source LLC
Chambersburg PA
CBHW071834210526
45479CB00001B/139